**Trading and Investing in the Forex Market
Using Chart Techniques**

For other titles in the Wiley Trading Series
please see www.wiley.com/finance

TRADING AND INVESTING IN THE FOREX MARKET USING CHART TECHNIQUES

G. A. Burgess

A John Wiley and Sons, Ltd., Publication

This edition first published 2009
© 2009 John Wiley & Sons, Ltd

Registered office
John Wiley & Sons Ltd, The Atrium, Southern Gate, Chichester, West Sussex, PO19 8SQ,
United Kingdom

For details of our global editorial offices, for customer services and for information about how to apply
for permission to reuse the copyright material in this book please see our website at www.wiley.com.

The right of the author to be identified as the author of this work has been asserted in accordance with
the Copyright, Designs and Patents Act 1988.

All rights reserved. No part of this publication may be reproduced, stored in a retrieval system, or
transmitted, in any form or by any means, electronic, mechanical, photocopying, recording or otherwise,
except as permitted by the UK Copyright, Designs and Patents Act 1988, without the prior permission of
the publisher.

Wiley also publishes its books in a variety of electronic formats. Some content that appears in print may
not be available in electronic books.

Designations used by companies to distinguish their products are often claimed as trademarks. All brand
names and product names used in this book are trade names, service marks, trademarks or registered
trademarks of their respective owners. The publisher is not associated with any product or vendor
mentioned in this book. This publication is designed to provide accurate and authoritative information in
regard to the subject matter covered. It is sold on the understanding that the publisher is not engaged in
rendering professional services. If professional advice or other expert assistance is required, the services
of a competent professional should be sought.

Library of Congress Cataloging-in-Publication Data

Burgess, Gareth.
  Trading and investing in the Forex market using chart techniques/Gareth Burgess.
    p. cm.
  Includes bibliographical references and index.
    ISBN 978-0-470-74527-4 (cloth : alk. paper)   1. Foreign exchange market.   2. Foreign exchange
futures.   3. Investment analysis.   4. Charts, diagrams, etc.   I. Title.
    HG3851.B866 2009
    332.4′5–dc22   2009015945

ISBN 978-0-470-74527-4

A catalogue record for this book is available from the British Library.

Typeset in 10/12pt Times by Aptara Inc., New Delhi, India.
Printed in Great Britain by TJ International Ltd, Padstow, Cornwall, UK

To
Piers Leslie

"A lie gets halfway around the world
before the truth has a chance to get its pants on"
—Winston Churchill

Contents

Preface		xi
1	**Candlesticks = Signals**	**1**
	Introduction	1
	Japanese Candlestick Signals	3
	The Single Signals	7
	Japanese Candlesticks – Double Candle Signals	32
	Some Candlestick Examples	47
	Some Further Candlestick Examples	47
	Chart Analysis Exercise 1	49
	Chart Analysis Exercise 1 – Answers	50
	Summary	50
2	**Chart Patterns = Opportunity**	**53**
	Continuation Patterns	54
	Reversal Patterns	54
	Bull Flags	54
	Bear Flags	54
	Bull Pennant	57
	Bear Pennant	57
	Bull Symmetrical Triangle	57
	Bear Symmetrical Triangle	57
	Bull Falling Wedge	63
	Bear Rising Wedge	65
	Inverted Head and Shoulders Continuation	66
	Part Two – Reversal Patterns	67
	Bullish Head and Shoulders Reversal Pattern	67
	Bearish Head and Shoulders Reversal Pattern	69
	Triple Top Pattern	69

Triple Bottom Pattern	69
The Double Top Pattern	72
The Double Bottom Pattern	72
The Bullish and Bearish "V" Pattern	72
Bullish "V" Top	77
Bearish "V" Bottom	77
The Broadening Top and Bottom	77
Some Chart Pattern Examples	81
Chart Analysis Exercise 2	82
Chart Analysis Exercise 2 – Answers	83
Summary	83
3 Buying and Selling = Support and Resistance Levels	**85**
Support and Resistance	86
Trend Lines	90
Trend Line Channels	90
Intermediate Trend Lines	95
Internal Trend Lines	96
Pivot Lines	96
Predetermined Pivot Highs and Lows	104
Calculated Pivot Lines	109
Fibonacci Levels	110
Chart Analysis Exercise 3	120
Chart Analysis Exercise 3 – Answers	121
Chart Analysis Exercise 4	122
Chart Analysis Exercise 4 – Answers	123
Summary	123
4 Applying Confirmation = Confidence Building	**125**
Simple Moving Average (SMA)	125
Simple Moving Average Channel	132
Chart Analysis Exercise 5	137
Chart Analysis Exercise 5 – Answers	138
Momentum Oscillators	139
The RSI Oscillator	140
The Stochastic Oscillator (Slow)	141
The MACD Oscillator	146
Chart Analysis Exercise 6	152
Chart Analysis Exercise 6 – Answers	153
Chart Analysis Exercise 6 – Answers (Continued)	154
Chart Analysis Exercise 7	155
Chart Analysis Exercise 7 – Answers	157
Summary	158

5	**Entry and Exit = Right or Wrong?**	**161**
	Climax Volume	162
	Pivot Lines as Entry and Exit	165
	High/Low/Close and High/Low Calculated Pivot Lines	170
	Candlesticks on Short-Term Charts	172
	Patterns on Short-Term Charts	174
	Summary	175
6	**Putting it all together = Practice and Patience**	**179**
	Finding the Technical Picture	180
	Creating the Watch List	190
	Money Management	193
	Summary	194
	A Word on Filters	194
	A Word on Recommendations	195
	Final Word	196
	Appendix	199
	Further Reading	201
	Index	203

Preface

People lie, charts do not, so when I pull up a chart onto my screen and apply techniques that help me interpret the price action of the market I feel more confident in my own ability to understand the financial markets and the financial industry as a whole. My judgement and decision making is therefore stronger because it is based on sound reasons that are not subject to someone else's mistakes or lies. I am alone with my business, but my business is stronger because I am at the heart of the decision-making process and do not have to rely on half-hearted attempts from others.

My first experience with charting began back in 1988, I used an Amstrad PC and spreadsheet software known then as Supercalc 3, to create a type of chart. It wasn't very successful but it was my first attempt at creating a chart. I didn't follow it any further because I went off to study at university. Since that time, however, I have visited various technical analysis courses and seminars, read some very useful books and some books that are a useless waste of valuable time. Since 1999, however, I have been drawing lines on charts as a professional and over the last five years I have invested a lot of my time in researching the financial markets.

Chart analysis, to me, as a method of interpreting market price action is actually a very efficient way of finding great investment opportunities. For the technical trader it is a method of finding the optimal point at which to enter the markets. The difficult part about charting, however, is the correct interpretation of price action and with so many techniques and signal based packages available today, it only goes to make the process of price interpretation even more complicated. I have researched many markets using certain ideas or a certain criteria believing that the more complicated the analysis the greater the success at trading. The more I searched and researched the more I have come to realise that the most suitable methods, at least those methods that suit my character, are the simplest methods. That is to say, trend lines, support and resistance levels, patterns, Japanese candlesticks, moving averages and in many cases Fibonacci based signals. All of which are very straightforward and visually very well displayed on a financial chart. To me these are the essential chart techniques necessary to find trade and investment opportunities in the financial markets today. For this reason they are compiled in this book.

All of these aspects of charting have one very significant and little thought about fact, they are the aftermath of market price action, therefore they do not rely on a system but instead your own interpretation of the price action; and because trading and investing is essentially the task of finding opportunities in the financial markets, chart analysis is about finding and confirming investment opportunities. The reason I believe this is that the markets are always trending either long term, intermediate term, short term and very short term i.e., intra-day. The advantage of this phenomenon is that you find a market where change is taking place and use the opportunity to go with it. A market that has been trending upwards changes and moves sideways, then changes again and moves down. In fact, that is all the markets do, they either go up or down, it's that simple. Yet for many traders and investors making consistent profits is anything but simple!

Likewise over the years I have seen how many traders and investors are too concerned about the immediate and fundamental aspect of the markets, listening to every piece of news and reading various recommendations that might help them determine the direction of the market for the next 100 or 200 pips, even if there are sufficient technical reasons that are pointing essentially to a market top. Given enough recommendations or positive news releases, it is enough to make traders and investors abandon their initial idea and fall into the trap of becoming unseated, disconcerted and then lost, resulting in poor performance.

Even when some traders are able to find sound investment ideas and initiate a good trade they tend to be disconcerted the moment the market moves against them, and change their opinion completely. I have also seen how many traders, especially those new to the business and those who trade in their spare time, do so without a plan and with the most complicated or flawed technical set up. Even if it is a short-term trade, by creating a plan based on the daily charts the short-term trading becomes easier and has more directional bias if the context of the bigger picture is understood. Quite simply, if there is a signal on the daily chart that the market is going to retrace the short-term trade should be interpreted with that direction in mind. Traders new to the business are often more interested in the reasons than trading the actual price.

The very nature of trading and investing makes this business difficult. The uncontrollable human emotions that rotate around greed, fear and hope are the elements of the human reaction in the markets that form the same repetitive scenarios time and time again. The need for some sort of confirmation or more useful methods is always at the forefront of investing, and when I came across Japanese candlesticks they seemed, at first, to be the answer. It was, however, after many attempts at trying to decipher candles that I realised they would not be the final part of the puzzle in my investment strategy, at least not applied on their own. I do make use of Japanese candlesticks as signals but they have to be confirmed and put into context. In this book they are used on a very basic level, but are an essential aspect of interpreting market sentiment visually.

Preface

The purpose of this book is to demonstrate how to find opportunities that present themselves as trade and investment opportunities. The signals, the warnings about market sentiment, and the context and confirmation of signals that are necessary will become apparent, and you will be introduced to some of the familiar chart techniques that have stood the test of time, examples made available in such a way that it will not take long to understand how to apply these techniques to your own charts and study them for market opportunities.

The financial markets do not care who you are or what you do but you care about the markets because you don't want to be treated badly by them for not having done your chart analysis properly. Remember, opportunities don't look you in the face every day, but when they do you should exploit them to the full. Chart technical analysis will help you do this, set strategically into the financial playing field where luck is not a fact! Finally, if you have experienced bad investments and wrong trade decisions you need to identify those factors that have undermined the investment and neutralise them. You will have to take steps to strengthen your decision process and become capable of resisting other challenges that might give rise to faulty decision making. This book will help you to at least see signals that are presenting a market that has an investment opportunity. They are clear and concise and therefore should help your decision-making process. If you feel, however, the need to look for advice by listening to other people, or other recommendations, then at least try to listen only to those people who have real trading experience!

ACKNOWLEDGEMENTS

First and foremost I would like to thank Caitlin Cornish for insight and suggestions during the draft stage of the book. I would also like to express my thanks to Aimee Dibbens, Samantha Hartley, Louise Holden and Lori Boulton at John Wiley & Sons. Thanks also to my copy editor Dan Leissner. Finally I would like to thank my wife Johanna, and my three wonderful children, Robin, Piers, and John-Jamie, for their understanding and patience during the writing of this book.

1
Candlesticks = Signals

INTRODUCTION

Traders and investors have been looking at charts for well over 85 years as Edwin Lefèvre wrote (1994, p. 61), "I should say that a chart helps those who can read it or rather who can assimilate what they read". The problem today, however, arises not only from the interpretation of the chart but also how best to apply the mass of indicators and what indicators are best applied.

This book and the techniques that are discussed set out to demonstrate how to use a chart in the context of the market price action, that is, what to look for on a financial chart and then to place the signal into some form of technical context that will make it possible to gain insight very quickly into a particular currency market, thus saving many hours of fundamental research. This book demonstrates chart analysis that can give you, as a technical trader, an edge for entering a position in the financial markets, allowing the position to be monitored on a daily basis for signs of change or weakness.

The purpose of this book is not to teach you how to trade the markets, but instead how to find opportunities in the markets that present themselves as trade and investment opportunities. The signals, the warnings about market sentiment become apparent once you understand how to apply some of the familiar chart techniques that have stood the test of time, examples made available in such a way that it will not take long to understand how to apply these techniques to your own charts and find trade and investment opportunities.

Regardless of whether you are a part-time trader or full-time trader, your only concern is to find important signals that represent opportunities that will lead you to a profit. The daily market price action that appears on charts in the form of Japanese candlesticks or patterns are, for whatever reason, the result of the actions of market participants, but a technical trader is not interested in the crowd's reasons for doing what they do, but instead the result of their buying and selling.

It is, however, during the buying and selling that the emotional responses of many market participants are heightened and these emotionally loaded responses to the market occur time and time again and are categorised as FEAR, HOPE and GREED. In light of the vast amount of information that is available via the internet or news channels, these emotions are quite often heightened to such an extent that it is almost impossible to make a clear decision leading in many cases to badly executed trades. The opinion of some expert somehow gets the message across that undermines your objective thinking, and it is ultimately the recommendation that is the technical trader's worst enemy. To invest in the financial markets it is absolutely necessary to create your own plan based on your own analysis. A trade should be executed from a position of power and confidence not from uncertainty or based on feelings.

In this book the techniques are applied in a relatively straightforward manner so as to create a technical picture on which to base an investment decision that does not rely on any outside recommendations but instead on your own visual analysis of the markets. A chart should be used to identify the opportunities that are ever present in the financial markets, monitor long-term investments and help to plan an investment decisively. Charts should also be used to find the appropriate level at which to enter or exit a position.

Chart analysis is a cold hard study of the markets, it is a study of the price action and nothing more. If the closing price of the Euro continues to move higher in the week then foreign exchange traders and investors will be buying that currency, which is a fact, in spite of what the fundamental and economical reasons may be.

Interpreting a chart is about recognising and understanding the sentiment of the market. If the market was bullish, is it still bullish, if not, why not? Is the market correcting or is it a reversal?

In this book, the more obvious techniques have been taken and applied as ideas for expressing the technical picture. The techniques have been arranged in order of importance and are readily and quickly understandable and bring those searching for a method of interpreting the financial markets to their objective.

Each subject relates to the phenomenon of chart technical analysis with the issue of the investment and trading strategy being part of the plan. Six primary chapters cover the subject matter.

Chapter 1 looks at the categories and ideas behind signals produced by Japanese candlesticks with a focus on the market sentiment. The candles are reduced to eight types in order to comprehend the ideas derived from them, covering the more general standard type signal representing both extreme and normal market conditions with the more abstract representing uncertainty and imminent change.

Chapter 2 relates to the patterns that appear in the financial markets and the various relationships to market sentiment including how to find possible measured targets upon a breakout of the pattern, a pause in the market trend and a change in market sentiment. Patterns are important signals and many market participants trade them.

Chapter 3 looks at the idea of support and resistance levels focusing on trend line support and resistance and the phenomena of polarity and pivot lines that give rise to a simple price observation at levels considered as bullish or bearish, allowing the technical trader to determine market direction and monitor positions.

Chapter 4 introduces the moving averages and the momentum indicators, both of which are based on the underlying price action. The averages supply information about the conditions of the market such as trending environment and support and resistance, the momentum indicators monitor the close in relation to the highs and lows over a set period of time and reflect this as the rate of change within the market. The momentum indicator is used for confirmation of market price action, displaying over-bought and over-sold conditions and divergence.

Chapter 5 applies certain techniques to the charts for finding optimal entry levels as confirmed by the techniques in the previous chapters. The obvious consequences of finding optimal market entry, covered by such themes as volume, pivot lines and interpretation of short-term charts, are very important for the technical trader.

Chapter 6, the final chapter, draws on all the methods and techniques discussed previously in order to create a plan not only for watching the markets for signals but also for developing a strategy to be used for investing and monitoring a position.

All of the methods and ideas covered here come under a form of classification in the world of technical analysis. There will be the view that the ideas contained here must include also the ideas relating to their class. This is not necessarily the case as there has to be an element of will in trading and investing. The operations that involve placing wealth at risk involve emotions, therefore all that can be achieved technically is to arrange those technical tools in accordance with the dominant ideas behind them and convey them in such a manner that the primary task of creating a consistent yet simple technical picture of the financial markets is achieved.

In studying these techniques the reader will undoubtedly try to adopt and produce slight variations. This should be encouraged, however, these techniques, especially those indicators used for the purpose of demonstrating a change in momentum, have stood the test of time, that is, they are universally accepted as being sufficient and do not require change or modification. Applying the same parameters and back testing will prove this argument. It is with these techniques that you will master the basics necessary to understand your own charts and thus read the underlying market sentiment.

JAPANESE CANDLESTICK SIGNALS

On Friday 13 July 2008, the foreign exchange cross EUR/JPY closed the week leaving a large bearish signal on the weekly candlestick chart. This signal, known as a "hanging man" in Japanese candlestick terms, is bearish if seen at certain levels on a chart especially after an advance in recent price action. It is considered by chartists and technical traders to be a warning that the market is reaching a top and may falter on attempts higher. This simple candlestick signal offered traders of the foreign exchange market (Forex or FX) a great opportunity to enter a short position in the EUR against the JPY, see Figure 1.1 overleaf.

(source MetaQuotes Software Corp)

Figure 1.1 EUR/JPY weekly chart with large hanging man candlestick.

The hanging man candlestick signal appeared on the chart because during the early part of the week the market had sold off sharply only to see buyers re-enter the market and push the price back towards the opening levels thus creating the "hanging man" with a lengthy "shadow".

At the close of that week there would have been many traders in the market, including fresh buyers, all of whom were anticipating higher levels to come and yet were nervous at the slightest decline in price action. The following week a similar candlestick appeared at the weekly close, another warning signal which left many forex traders that weekend concerned about their positions in the market. Two weeks after the first hanging man appeared, clues begin to unfold which confirmed that there is a change taking place in the market, a change which the initial bearish candlestick had signalled previously. For example, there was a close below the current trend line that week, the first since the trend began on 16 March 2008, that is 19 weeks had passed before the trend line had been violated! Another very important clue was the close of that weekly candlestick on Friday 25 July 2008, this was the first weekly close at the 10-week moving average level since the two averages crossed positive on 18 May 2008. In fact, prices dipped below the 10-week moving average before closing just above it but still below the trend line, see Figure 1.2 opposite.

Candlesticks = Signals 5

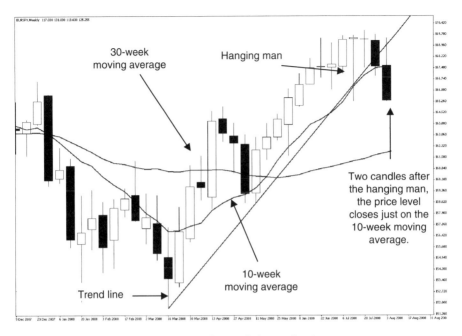

(source MetaQuotes Software Corp)

Figure 1.2 EUR/JPY weekly chart demonstrating a break of a trend line and a close below the 10-week moving average, the market sentiment is changing.

At this point those traders that had entered the market pushing the market back up would have been left holding losing positions but still hanging on in hope that the market would move off higher from the current level. Although the EUR/JPY cross did attempt to move higher from the 10-week moving average it was rejected, not only from the highs, but also from the trend line where technical traders had been waiting to sell, see Figure 1.3 overleaf.

The hanging man candlestick signal now began to take effect. At some point, those traders, either working in banks or large corporate organisations that were still long began to reduce their exposure in the market by cutting the size of their positions. The result of all of this is that the EUR/JPY cross accelerates lower as traders cut their positions. As you can see from the chart in Figure 1.4 overleaf, the price pauses at the 30-week moving average before continuing much lower. Originally, all of this price action was based on a very powerful and yet very visual signal.

There were also two other very important clues that the EURO would struggle to move higher against the Japanese Yen. The stochastic indicator was in the over-bought zone and was beginning to cross negative, there was also a large triangle pattern from which the EUR/JPY had broken out too soon, suggesting that prices would falter and find their way back inside the triangle.

6   Trading and Investing in the Forex Market Using Chart Techniques

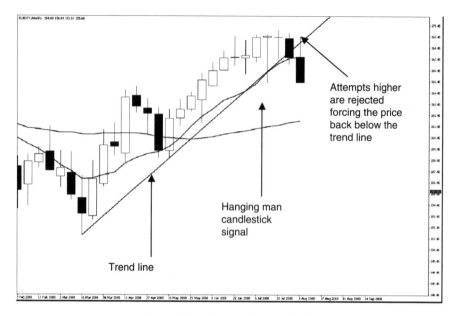

(source MetaQuotes Software Corp)

Figure 1.3 EUR/JPY weekly chart showing the beginning of break down in market price action.

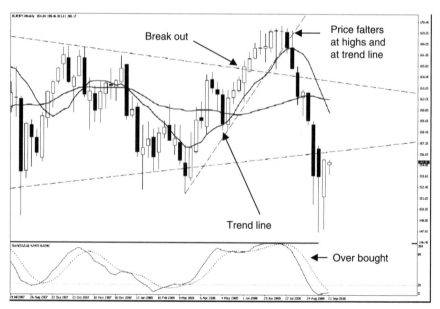

(source MetaQuotes Software Corp)

Figure 1.4 EUR/JPY weekly chart after the break down in market price action has occurred.

Candlesticks = Signals 7

(source MetaQuotes Software Corp)

Figure 1.5 USD/CAD daily chart showing buy and sell areas.

Having seen the hanging man candlestick signal, you as a technical trader of the foreign exchange market would have been prepared for a change in market sentiment. You would have expected the change to happen and would have been watching the chart for further technical evidence to confirm the signal, gathering information and creating a strategy from your chart that would enable you technically to follow the market. What is probably more important, however, is the trade which you would have seen as a low risk trade in your favour. A stop loss order placed some points above the hanging man, at the level where you would have been wrong and wanted to protect your money, was easily positioned in the market, ensuring absolute risk/reward.

A chart should be technically easy to interpret. If the technical picture is difficult to understand then something is wrong with your analysis or some technical indicator has not been placed correctly on the chart. It is the signals together with indicators as well as support and resistance and trend lines that make up the technical picture that helps to dissect the market price action and display the market sentiment in such a way that a conclusion may be reached, see Figure 1.5. These techniques must be consistent and concise in their application. Consistency will help to avoid uncertainty in finding and confirming the opportunities as and when they appear on the chart.

THE SINGLE SIGNALS

Beginning with Japanese candlesticks, these signals originate with a Japanese rice merchant named Munehisa Homma (also known as Sokyu Honma) (1724–1803), who developed a graphical set of rules to use for trading rice. It is from this period in Japan that candlesticks as we understand them today are derived. A candlestick is a graphical representation of the OPEN, HIGH, LOW and CLOSE of the market price action and for this reason it is very important to have accurate data. Candlesticks that have a 22:00 GMT close on the foreign exchange market (after the New York close) may have slightly different graphical implications compared to a candle that has a 23:00 GMT close or a midnight (GMT) close. Graphically, candlesticks display market sentiment in such a way that makes the task of sifting through charts easier. They are usually coloured to represent the direction, for example, a higher close relative to the open might be white, a lower close relative to the open may be black. This has the advantage of recognising the day's trading at a glance, i.e., a negative day or a positive day, see Exhibit 1.1.

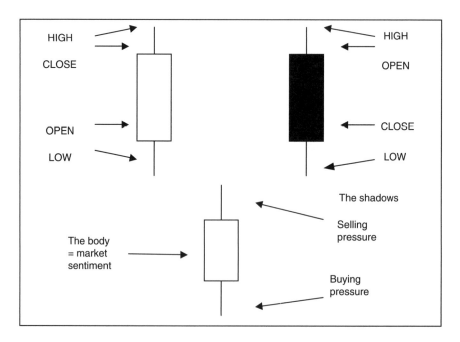

Exhibit 1.1 White candle is a positive, the market price action moved up throughout the day; the black candle is a negative day, here the market price moved down.

The candlestick chart is a visual representation of the inner workings of a market. The selling pressure or the buying pressure is displayed visually allowing for immediate insight into the market. The candlestick shadows are useful as indicators of resistance and support, allowing lines to be drawn on the chart with relative ease at these levels. It is, however, the market sentiment and change in market sentiment that candlesticks charts demonstrate best. Simply compare a bar chart to a candlestick chart and this becomes apparent.

Candlesticks = Signals

(source MetaQuotes Software Corp)

Figure 1.6 EUR/GBP daily chart with some examples of Japanese candlestick signals displaying the market sentiment as bullish or bearish.

The daily candlestick chart shown in Figure 1.6 displays the same price information as the daily bar chart in Figure 1.7 overleaf. Where the candlestick chart displays the sentiment of the market the bar chart says very little until the market breaks out of its range or channel or makes a new high or low.

A bar chart, as compared to a candlestick chart, can display patterns and channels more clearly than a candlestick chart and this is probably a bar chart's greatest advantage. However, the visual clues about daily market sentiment are not so easy to discern. Where as a candlestick that opened at the lows and moved higher, closing at the highs, is demonstrating that the market has been positive, a candlestick that has opened, found support and closed only slightly higher during the course of the session is demonstrating uncertainty in the market. These variations are displayed very well visually on a candlestick chart but not on bar charts.

Applying candlesticks to the chart it is not only possible to establish the day's range as with a bar chart, but also establish the sentiment of that range by looking at the body of the candlestick that forms between the open and the close. A positive day has seen more buying than selling, perhaps large orders going through the market,

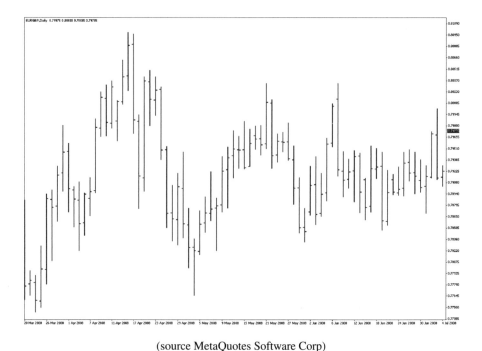

(source MetaQuotes Software Corp)

Figure 1.7 Example of a EUR/GBP daily bar chart with very little to see about what the market sentiment is in this market.

and many short-term traders decide on a direction. A negative day is just the opposite; the session has seen more sellers than buyers with many buyers just sitting on the sidelines. An uncertain day, however, is a sign that the market has seen many buyers or sellers quickly finding resistance or support and those buyers or sellers that did enter that session may have exited the market very quickly thereafter. These are days where the market consolidates.

Japanese candlesticks applied to a chart on their own are not the solution to understanding the financial markets. Candlesticks can often be interpreted falsely especially as many of them look like reversal signals. Many investors and technical traders do not apply them on charts for exactly this reason. Another reason that many professional investors find candlesticks difficult is that the daily session may trade at the same level for 90 % of the day; the market can trade around a certain price level for most of the session only to move higher towards the close of the session, the real body is arguably not representative of the real trading session. It is, therefore, necessary to look at the short-term time frame in order to confirm that this has happened and find the bulk of the trading on the 60 min. chart so as to clear up any uncertainty, see Exhibit 1.2 opposite.

Candlesticks = Signals

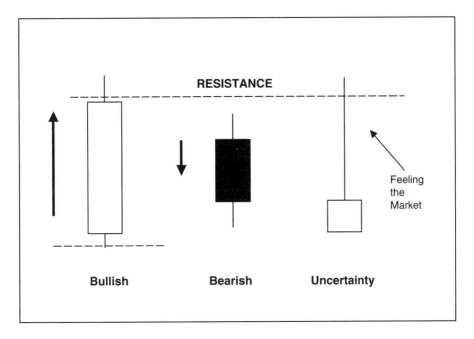

Exhibit 1.2 White candle is positive, black candle is negative, long shadow found strong selling pressure.

The close of the session is important and for this reason, as will be demonstrated later in this book, it is necessary to place candlesticks within the context of other indicators and in particular to find a significant level on the chart and then watch to see if the market is closing at, above or below the level of importance. This is a useful indication of a truly bullish, bearish or uncertain market. Put simply, to watch how the market reacts at certain pre-defined levels and observe what type of candlestick forms at these levels.

For the purpose of this book the candlesticks in Exhibit 1.3, on page 13, are constructed to follow a system of classification of signals that is expressible by the open, close, high and low of the market session. The main aim is to obtain the greatest amount of visual utility. Therefore the arrangement has been adapted accordingly to the simplest and most visual form that appears on daily charts, one that will not require a deep comprehension of Japanese candlesticks. These candlestick signals are the more obvious signals which best reflect market sentiment at a glance. The objective is to learn to recognise the signals that candlesticks produce with regard to the sentiment of the market and the change in market sentiment, which is what you as a technical trader and investor should be concerned with because where there is change, there is opportunity!

As a guide, it is useful to see the white candles as positive and the black candles as negative, as well as the size and frequency which should be noted on the chart.

(source MetaQuotes Software Corp)

Figure 1.8 EUR/GBP weekly chart with positive days, negative days and uncertain days.

A white positive candle may still have bearish implications and a black negative candle with a long shadow may only be a pause in market price action before the market continues higher, and is thus positive overall. A negative closing hammer that appears at support only to see a positive session thereafter could be seen as having even stronger bullish implications. It is therefore necessary to apply confirmation as much as possible. Where the real body of the candle can show market sentiment, the highs and lows are just as important. Higher lows suggest greater buying interest and lower highs just the opposite.

Candlestick signals form the basis of chart reading in this book and are discussed as signals in the light of other techniques that confirm the signal. More often than not candlestick signals provide a very early warning about a possible change in market sentiment. Occasionally, however, a candlestick may take a few days before the change in market sentiment actually begins to unfold.

This is particularly important when reading charts with candlesticks. Learn to see how often a harami actually unfolds in the next session and how often it requires a

Candlesticks = Signals 13

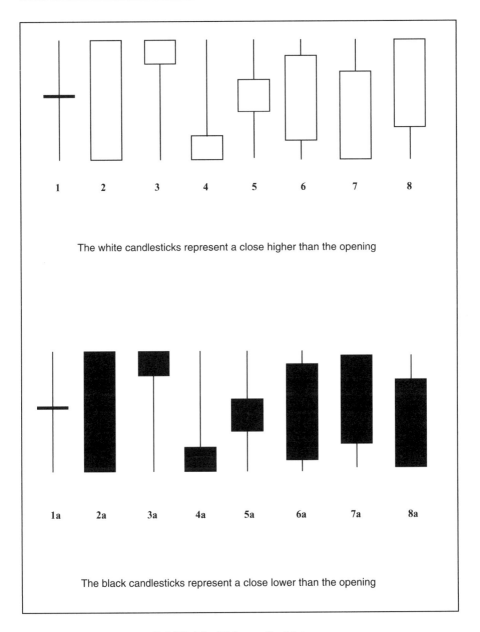

Exhibit 1.3 Eight candlestick types.

few days before that signal begins to unfold. Together with other important technical aspects these signals will prove to be very valuable. Finally, rather than back test candlestick patterns simply take a chart and look for these candlesticks, see how the market reacts to them.

1. Doji Cross – Opens and closes at same level = warning uncertain market.
2. Marabozu – Opens at the lows, closes at the highs = positive market.
3. Hammer – Opens, finds buying pressure, closes higher = positive market.
4. Inverted Hammer – Opens at the lows, moves higher, finds sellers, closes near open = warning (can be black or white in colour).
5. Spinning Top – Opens, finds support and resistance, closes higher = uncertainty
6. Standard day – Opens, moves lower, finds support, closes near highs = positive market.
7. Bullish Belt-Hold Line – Opens at support, moves higher, finds resistance, closes near to highs = continuation.
8. Bullish Closing Bozu – Opens, moves lower, finds good support, closes at the highs = positive.

1a. Doji Cross – Open and closed at same level = warning uncertain market.
2a. Marabozu – Opens at high, closes at the low = negative market.
3a. Hanging Man – Selling pressure with a close lower than the opening.
4a. Shooting Star – Buyers found support, pressure causes lower close (can be black or white in colour).
5a. Spinning Top – Opens, moves lower, finds support, moves higher, finds resistance, closes lower than open = uncertainty
6a. Standard Line – Opens, moves higher, finds resistance, moves lower, finds support, closes near to the lows.
7a. Bearish Belt-Hold Line – Opens at resistance and immediately moves lower closing near the lows.
8a. Bearish Closing Bozu – Opens, moves higher, finds good resistance, closes at the low of the day = Negative.

Candlestick 1 and 1a, the Doji Candlestick

This candlestick is very well known amongst technical traders and is a very important signal. Should this be seen after a recent advance in price action it is a warning that the market may have reached a turning point, that there is a possible change in market sentiment, a pause at the very least. This type of candle can have very long shadows with no body or very short shadows with no body. The trading session has seen very little progress with many short-term traders becoming confused, leading to uncertainty in the market.

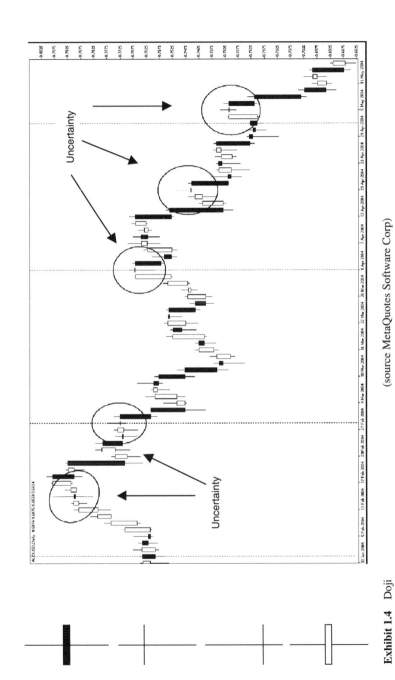

Figure 1.9 AUS/USD daily chart with Doji candlesticks signalling a possible change in market direction. (source MetaQuotes Software Corp)

Exhibit 1.4 Doji type candles.

The doji candlestick has variations. The shadow can be longer or shorter and the open and close may be at one end of the shadow, which is known as a gravestone doji (bearish) or dragonfly doji (bullish). It is the warning signal which these candlesticks display visually that signals opportunities for the technical trader.

Candlestick 2 and 2a, the Marabozu Candlestick

The long candle that is known as a marabozu candlestick which opens at the low and closes at the high signals a very positive market session. This candlestick has no upper and lower shadow and although not crucial in the FX markets, is often characteristic of this type of candlestick. The candlestick can also stand out as being abnormally large in comparison to a normal daily session and can be two to three times the length. The market has experienced a large move and is likely to retrace due to profit taking. This candlestick can appear in the opposite direction to the main trend but the mid point becomes an area to watch for support or resistance (which is useful as a point of reference for future price action as these levels can often be important for long periods).

The example in Figure 1.11 on page 18 demonstrates how useful these candlesticks can be as a point of reference for future price levels that are likely to see some sort of reaction around the mid point of the body. These levels on charts are known as support and resistance levels that become pivotal, that is, these levels indicate price zones that are support or resistance until broken at which point an area that has seen resistance will become support or support then becomes resistance. Figure 1.11 demonstrates quite well how the mid-point can be applied as an area of future support or resistance. The candlestick in Figure 1.11 is an excellent example of a resistance level in progress; tested and validated on various occasions the line of resistance becomes an important level for the technical trader. In this example, the level is generated from the mid point of the candlestick, but pivot lines can be found and generated in different ways. These methods are discussed in Chapter 3 and form an important aspect of charting.

Candlestick 3, the Hammer

The hammer candlestick as a signal appears after a decline in price action. It is discernible by the large shadow that appears below the small body. The price action has been in decline, perhaps for weeks, until it becomes exhaustive culminating in one final sell off. For the most part, a significant area of support has been found that should already be on the chart. The market touches the point where buyers see the market as an opportunity, together with those market participants who are buying back their short positions. The price is forced back towards and finally above the opening level. This can happen relatively quickly.

The hammer signal may not always be as conclusive as in Figure 1.12 on page 19, but its appearance suggests that the selling pressure is over and that the market

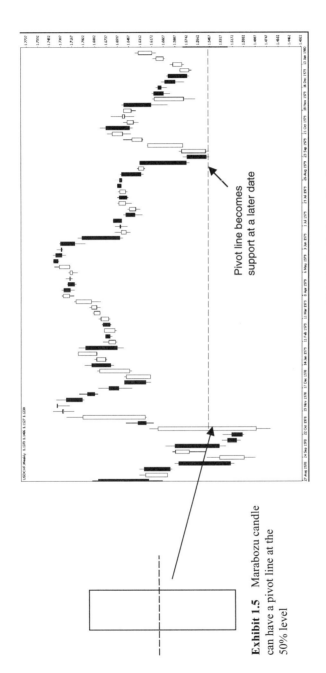

Exhibit 1.5 Marabozu candle can have a pivot line at the 50% level

Figure 1.10 USD/CHF Weekly chart showing a candle three times the length of a typical daily candle. There is often some retracement during the following sessions as profit is removed. The approximate centre of the candle usually provides a good level of support and resistance.

(source MetaQuotes Software Corp)

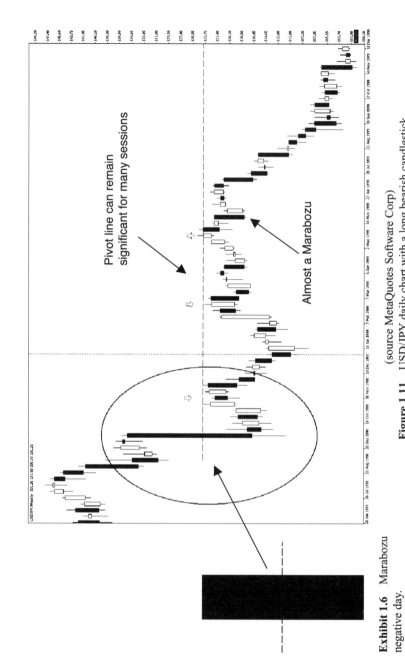

Figure 1.11 USD/JPY daily chart with a long bearish candlestick. (source MetaQuotes Software Corp)

Exhibit 1.6 Marabozu negative day.

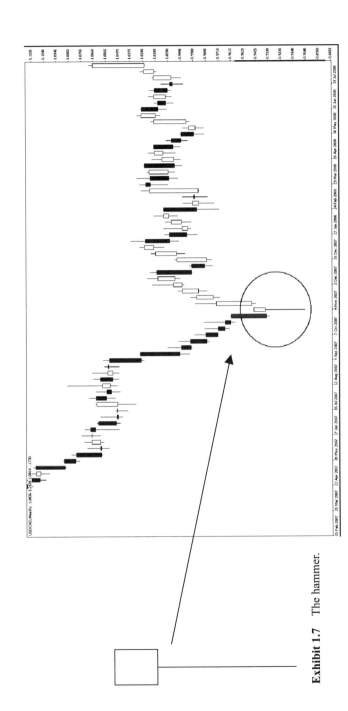

Figure 1.12 USD/CAD weekly chart displaying the end of a bearish trend with the appearance of bullish hammer signalling a possible change.

(source MetaQuotes Software Corp)

Exhibit 1.7 The hammer.

is turning bullish. The colour of the body can also be black, signalling a weaker close, but discrimination should be applied in order to determine the importance of the level that the market price action has reached. A white body has a higher close and would suggest a more bullish sentiment.

Candlestick 3a, the Hanging Man

This type of signal, known as the hanging man, is like the hammer signal unique in that a lengthy shadow appears under the real body of the candle, but unlike the hammer candlestick the hanging man is seen after a recent advance in price action. The market experiences a sell off only to see buyers re-enter the market and push the price back towards the opening levels. This candlestick has bearish implications. As with all candlestick signals that imply a top or bottom, confirmation techniques should be used to determine the significance of the level that the price has reached.

Candlestick 4, the Shooting Star

This signal appears at market tops. The shooting star is signalling a potential loss of momentum as the market finds selling pressure. Those buyers that have been in the market for the medium term together with the short-term buyers begin to take profits resulting in a sharp sell off that leaves many intra-day buyers exiting their positions quickly. The body can be black or white but whereas the inverted hammer is a signal that appears at market bottoms this signal is seen at market tops. Caution should be applied to this signal as it can imply continuation; interestingly this signal at fresh highs can be informative in as much as it suggests that there is bullish sentiment in the market, but that first attempts into uncharted territory resulted in selling pressure. Again, finding and waiting for confirmation is important with this signal. The example in Figure 1.14 on page 22 shows that the following session resulted in a negative day that confirms the shooting star signal.

Candlestick 4a, the Inverted Hammer

The inverted hammer found at market bottoms is similar to the hanging man found at market tops. The body of the candlestick is small and there is a large shadow above the real body. The market has found support and turned bullish. Many market participants who were short on previous sessions will have quickly had their positions stopped out, thereby forcing the market higher. The movement, however, is flawed as no fresh buyers enter at this level and many of those who stepped in forcing the price up during the intra day move quickly take profits and sit on the sidelines. The signal is, however, a useful indication of a possible change in market direction. As with the example in Figure 1.15 on page 23, it takes three further sessions before the market becomes confidently bullish. Unlike the hammer at market tops, this signal at market bottoms often requires more buying pressure to push prices higher than the hammer requires selling pressure to move a market lower.

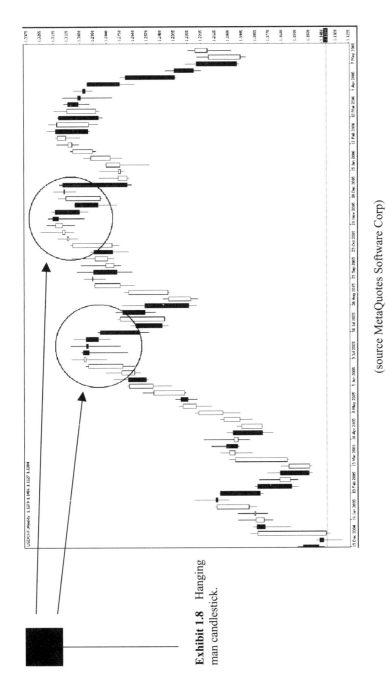

Exhibit 1.8 Hanging man candlestick.

Figure 1.13 USD/CHF weekly chart with two hammers appearing after an advance in price action and warning of a change in market sentiment. (source MetaQuotes Software Corp)

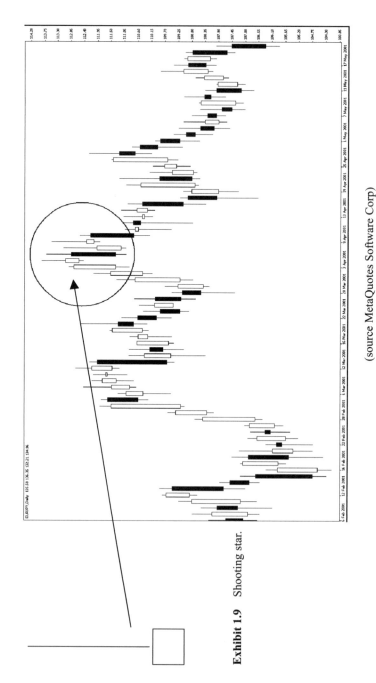

Figure 1.14 EUR/JPY daily chart showing that a shooting star selling pressure has been found but which can also imply a continuation in bullish price action.

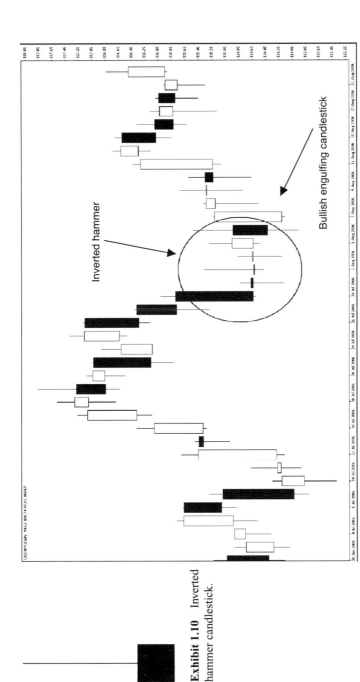

Figure 1.15 USD/JPY daily chart with inverted hammer as an early warning about a possible change in market direction. Four sessions later a bullish engulfing session finally produces the key day but the inverted hammer warns of a possible change in direction, at the least you would not want to be thinking about being short.

(source MetaQuotes Software Corp)

Exhibit 1.10 Inverted hammer candlestick.

Candlestick 5 and 5a, the Spinning Top

This candlestick usually signifies a pause in market direction. The market has moved higher and lower throughout the day's session, but the real body of the candlestick is small. This suggests that the market session has been range bound with no real commitment in either direction. The small body with shadows suggests that the short-term market participants are uncertain, their positions are quickly stopped out during the session. Typically many traders will sit on the sidelines and wait for a clearer signal.

A market that is experiencing a pause or consolidation will display this in the form of a row of spinning tops. Eventually a break out will occur and the move thereafter can be quite substantial. Find a chart with four or five spinning tops in a row and it might be worth watching intently for the break out rather than trying to categorise or figure out what the Japanese pattern might be. The trend will tend to dominate so a row of spinning tops in an up trend would suggest that the break out will be in the direction of the trend.

Candlestick 6 and 6a, Standard Candlestick

This candlestick is seen as a standard positive session. The market found support and then moved higher throughout the session closing near the highs. It is an important candle in a trending market as it signifies and confirms a healthy market. In a trending market buyers will be watching the high of these sessions for confirmation that the market will continue higher. Small body candlesticks follow the standard candlestick in the example chart below, suggesting that traders are cautious but remain bullish as seen by the fact that there are more white candlestick bodies than black candlestick bodies, that is, more positive than negative daily closes.

Candlestick 7, Bullish Belt-Hold Line

The bullish belt-hold line signal suggests support. This signal appearing at a base or towards the end of a range suggests that the market is turning bullish going forward. From the opening the market moves higher but does not close at the highs. The support level on this type of candle is quite strong and could be sufficient enough to place a support line or pivot line on the chart for future reference. If the opening area is already at a support level from the previous market action then this type of candle will confirm the level.

Such candles, if seen at levels of support, add confidence to your strategy. As long as the support level remains valid the bullish belt-hold line suggests that the market sentiment is holding. This may require watching for further signals to support this but, as in Figure 1.18 on page 27, a hammer candlestick appears after which the market does not touch the support level again and only moves higher.

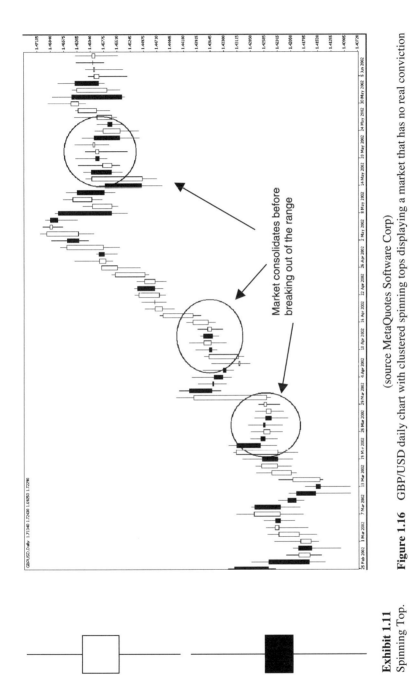

Figure 1.16 GBP/USD daily chart with clustered spinning tops displaying a market that has no real conviction and is pausing. (source MetaQuotes Software Corp)

Exhibit 1.11
Spinning Top.

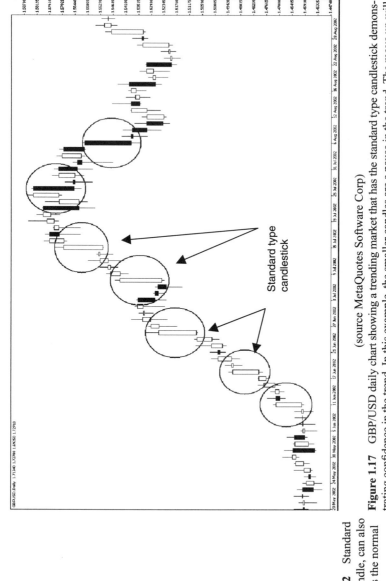

Exhibit 1.12 Standard day type candle, can also be 2/3 times the normal daily size.

Figure 1.17 GBP/USD daily chart showing a trending market that has the standard type candlestick demonstrating confidence in the trend. In this example, the smaller candles are a pause in the trend. The move up will have seen positive market sentiment but this slows and short-term traders become uncertain. In this type of scenario it is preferable to remain with the direction of the trend in anticipation of a move higher to come.

(source MetaQuotes Software Corp)

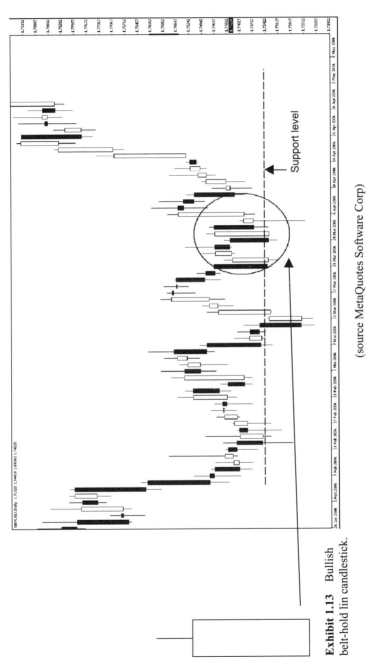

Exhibit 1.13 Bullish belt-hold lin candlestick.

(source MetaQuotes Software Corp)

Figure 1.18 GBP/USD daily chart with a bullish belt-holdline. Sometimes the initial signal can take a few more sessions before it has the desired effect.

Candlestick 7a, Bearish Belt-Hold Line

This signal appears at tops and bottoms. The appearance at market tops is useful for indicating that the resistance level is valid. The open is at or very close to a resistance level from which the price actions move away. As in the example shown in Figure 1.19 opposite, the bearish belt-hold line opens just below the close of the previous sessions, down past the opening and into the shadow of the previous session, suggesting that support is waning!

The opening is at a level which may have seen resistance for many previous sessions, it may also require that the level be found by searching the price history for some technical aspect that occurred and which still has some significance. Support and resistance levels can have an important role on charts for many days, weeks, months and even years.

In the example in Figure 1.19, the candle opened at the resistance level and moved away thus confirming the level as resistance. Another particularly good signal that is generated by this type of candle is when it appears at market highs. The signal then suggests the complete opposite to its standard usage. The chart in Figure 1.20 demonstrates this quite well. The session has a positive start evidenced by the fact that it moves higher from the session. The support is confirmed and many traders will be bullish especially as the market has been trending. However, the shooting star (inverted hammer), two sessions earlier, contains the bullish activity within its shadows. The belt-hold candlestick has pushed up into an area of resistance as it moves towards the high of the shooting star!

Another example of combining candles and finding confirmation is shown by the bearish belt-hold line in Figure 1.20 on page 30. The belt-hold candle opens at a marabozu pivot line which confirms the belt-hold candle. If you were short-term trading and you saw the price moving down from the opening and you already had the resistance level marked on your chart you would be cautious about buying the market at that level!

Candlestick 8, Bullish Closing Bozu

The bullish closing bozu is a signal that should be seen as an opportunity to monitor the strength of the market. Closing at the highs is considered to be positive going forward; this signal, however, can often be the beginning of a reversal! The most useful way to utilise this signal is when it appears in a trending environment, then monitor the opening of the next session. If the market has been moving higher and this candle appears the chances are that the market price action will continue. If, however, the same candle signal appears during a down trend but there is no reason to believe that a base has been found, then it suggests that the market will continue to move lower. At which point the base, i.e., the support level will become resistance once broken. The price action of the following session should have little or no activity below the close. It is very important to watch the price level for the following session. Likewise, for a base confirmed by other techniques – as in Figure 1.21 on page 31 – which has

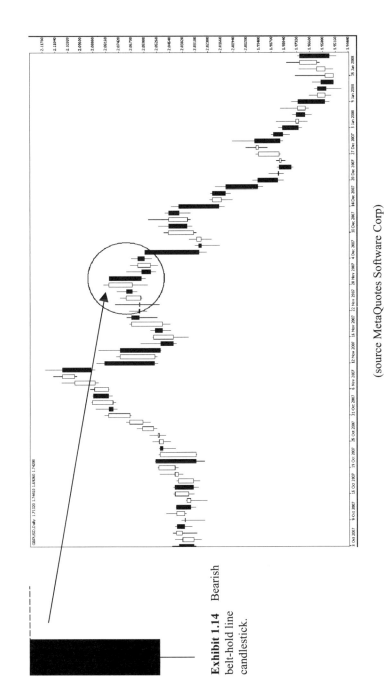

Exhibit 1.14 Bearish belt-hold line candlestick.

Figure 1.19 GBP/USD daily chart with a bearish belt-hold line at resistance.
(source MetaQuotes Software Corp)

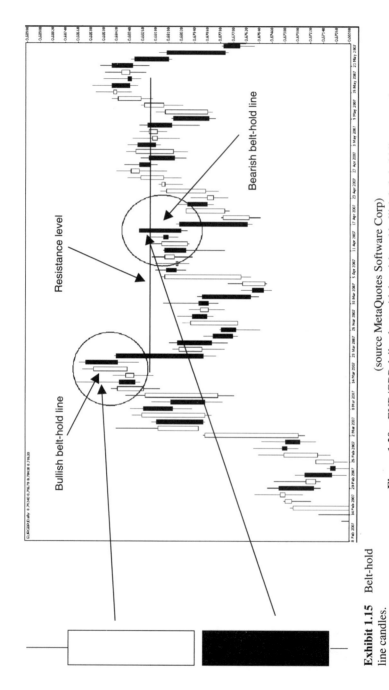

Exhibit 1.15 Belt-hold line candles.

Figure 1.20 EUR/GBP daily chart with bearish and bullish belt-hold line examples. (source MetaQuotes Software Corp)

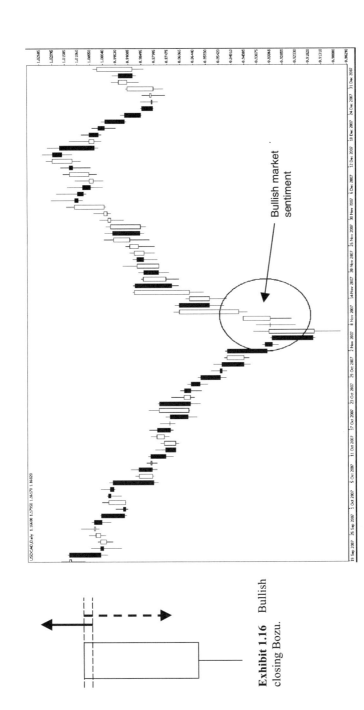

Exhibit 1.16 Bullish closing Bozu.

Figure 1.21 USD/CAD daily chart with a bullish closing bozu. (source MetaQuotes Software Corp)

seen a bullish engulfing day and then a pause which sees a bullish closing bozu that helps confirm the base.

Candlestick 8a, Bearish Closing Bozu

The same applies to the bearish closing bozu in that this candlestick helps to confirm the market sentiment as being a continuation of the ongoing or immediate trend. This signal requires confirmation in order to continue having confidence in the continuation of a trend. One simple method, as with the bullish closing bozu, is to monitor the opening of the next session. Too much time above the middle of the bozu candlestick body suggests that the price action will reverse. It is a sign that the market might need more time before it has the expected impact on market price action.

There are other techniques which are discussed later in this book that could be applied to the chart in Figure 1.22 on page 33, and that would enable the technical trader to confirm the sentiment of the market generated by the closing bozu candlestick signal.

JAPANESE CANDLESTICKS – DOUBLE CANDLE SIGNALS

There are also candlestick patterns that require a previous candle for comparison. The candlesticks are the same as the eight single candlesticks at the beginning of this chapter, but are interpreted by looking at the impact of the opening of the new candle against the range of the previous candle, especially the closing price of the previous candle. This is useful for observing any change in market sentiment that might be occurring. One technique for an early sign of a reversal is to look at the close of the present candle against the opening of the previous candle.

The Bullish Engulfing Pattern

Candlestick signals require confirmation in order to support the initial signals that are generated and the methods and techniques of doing this are discussed later in this book. However, comparing candlesticks to the previous candlestick can be very useful in observing change in market sentiment and confirming the current price level as supportive or as resistance. The bullish engulfing pattern, for example, is a strong reversal signal. When these two candles appear it suggests that a significant support level has been found. The signal is produced when the previous candlestick body is engulfed. The criterion is for an opening to be below the previous candlestick's close and the closing of the current session to be above the previous candlestick's open. As with the bullish closing bozu candle in Figure 1.23 on page 35, not only is that candle itself bullish but together with the previous candles it also forms an engulfing session. A close at the highs is positive going forward.

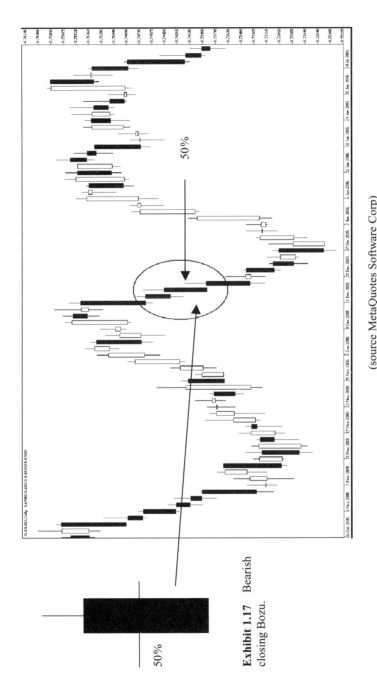

Exhibit 1.17 Bearish closing Bozu.

Figure 1.22 AUS/USD daily chart with a bearish closing bozu. (source MetaQuotes Software Corp)

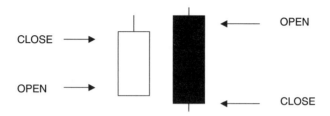

Exhibit 1.18 The current range against the previous range.

The Bearish Engulfing Pattern

This is the opposite of the bullish engulfing pattern. Again, this signal forms at areas of strong resistance. The opening should be above the previous close and the close should end the session below the previous open. The candlestick type that engulfs the previous session is equally important. Shown in the example below, the single candle in Figure 1.24 on page 36 is a bearish belt-hold line candle! The session has opened at the highs and moved lower right through the previous session's trading. This candle can confirm that there is now strong resistance at that level. The belt-hold line engulfs the previous session thus confirming a bearish engulfing pattern. This candle not only confirms resistance at the opening but engulfs the entire body of the previous session. This represents quite a strong change in market sentiment.

The Piercing Pattern

This is a similar pattern to the engulfing pattern but does not have the same strength of signalling of a correction as the engulfing pattern. The appearance of the piercing pattern is a warning that support has been found but that confirmation is necessary with this pattern. This signal is generated when the price action retraces to at least 50 % of the previous session. This candlestick signal forms at the lows, finds support and then moves back through the opening and higher into the body of the previous session. The candlestick should pierce the previous session by at least 50 %. The further the penetration the stronger the signal!

Dark Cloud Cover

The opposite candlestick to the piercing pattern is the dark cloud cover pattern. This candlestick forms at the highs of a move and is often seen after a recent advance in price action. The deeper this candle penetrates the previous body the greater the significance the pattern has as a turning signal.

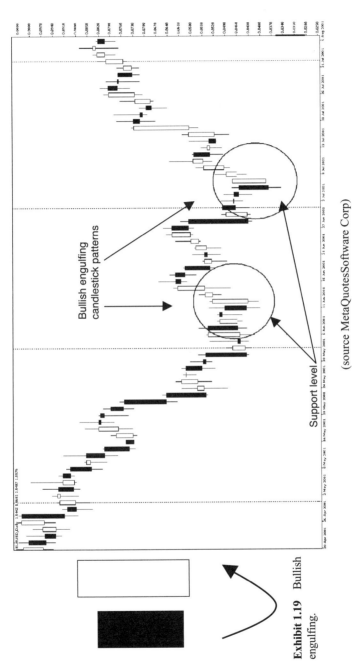

Figure 1.23 GBP/USD daily chart showing a bullish engulfing candlestick that opens below the previous close and finishes the session above the previous open. (source MetaQuotesSoftware Corp)

Exhibit 1.19 Bullish engulfing.

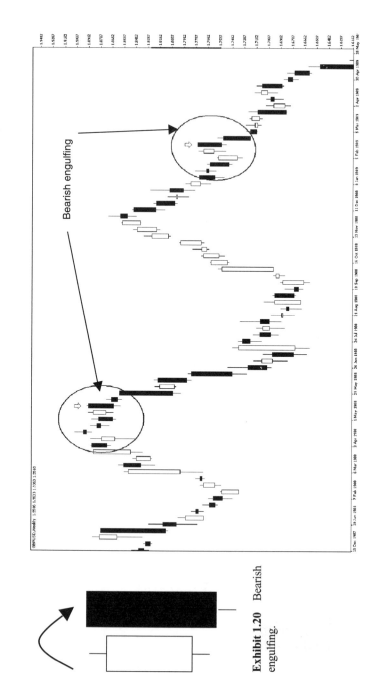

Figure 1.24 GBP/USD daily chart showing a bearish engulfing pattern created by a belt-hold line candlestick. There is a similar pattern known as an outside day on the bar chart. The market has been trending before encountering resistance. The price makes a new high and quickly retraces the previous session closing below the previous session's opening level.

(source MetaQuotes Software Corp)

Exhibit 1.20 Bearish engulfing.

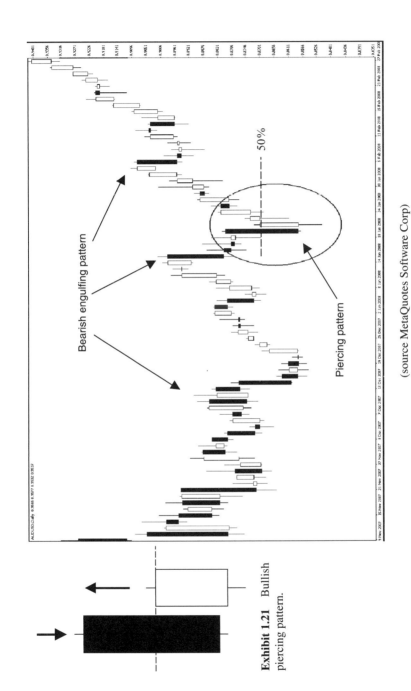

Exhibit 1.21 Bullish piercing pattern.

Figure 1.25 AUS/USD daily chart showing bearish engulfing pattern and a (bullish) piercing pattern. (source MetaQuotes Software Corp)

This is not quite as bearish as an engulfing pattern but with the forex market the close and open are not as definable as a market that has a 10-hour gap between the close and the open. Many forex traders will simply be trading from what they have seen earlier on in the day regardless of what the time is.

Figure 1.26 opposite demonstrates quite well the significance of the dark cloud cover candlestick.

The Tweezer Top

This signal forms when the price action finds resistance for two consecutive sessions. The tweezer top signal is bearish and using this candlestick formation together with an engulfing pattern it is a very useful technique that has great visual advantages for finding resistance levels on charts at a glance. The second session does not have to engulf the body of the previous session but if it does it is very strong. Those traders and investors who were long from the previous session will now be on the wrong side of the market. The market may not have been trending and can be a range bound market when this occurs, but either way the highs of both candles must falter at or almost at the same level of resistance.

The tweezer pattern can have many variations, for example a tweezer harami, a tweezer dark cloud cover or a tweezer engulfing. The level at which the two candles form is important.

The Tweezer Bottom

As with the tweezer top signalling a strong resistance level, the tweezer bottom signifies an important support level. The low from the previous session remains supportive and the price action therefore moves higher. A tweezer candlestick set up can be made up of various candlestick types as long as the lows or highs are at the same level and usually with both showing the shadows at the same level. Those traders who went short on the previous session are now forced out of their positions and are likely to sit at the side. An engulfing session, for example, would be a powerful tweezer combination, as shown in the example in Figure 1.28 on page 41.

The tweezer pattern is a very distinctive signal and stands out on the chart especially if there are long shadows on both candles.

The Harami Top

The harami signal appears as a warning that the market sentiment of the prior trend may be changing. This candle signal is quite powerful in displaying the uncertainty of the market; confirmation is required with this pattern as the harami can often be a pause before the market continues higher. If the market is trending very strongly then common sense will dictate that the harami may simply be a pause in the market rather than a turning signal.

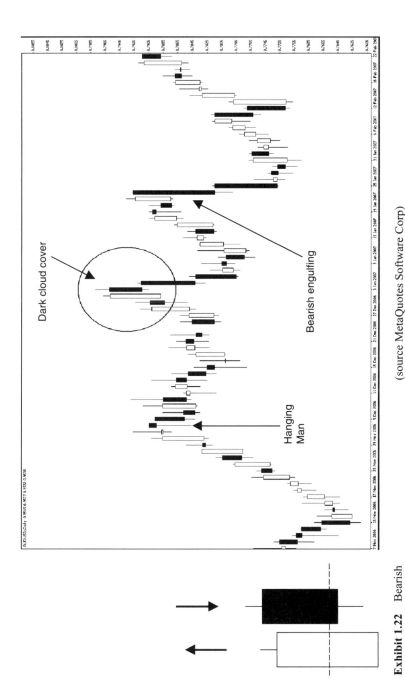

Figure 1.26 AUS/USD daily chart showing a dark cloud cover candlestick pattern. (source MetaQuotes Software Corp)

Exhibit 1.22 Bearish piercing pattern.

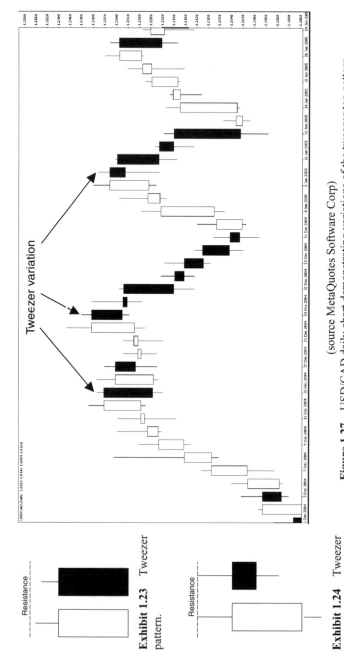

Figure 1.27 USD/CAD daily chart demonstrating variations of the tweezer top pattern. (source MetaQuotes Software Corp)

Exhibit 1.23 Tweezer pattern.

Exhibit 1.24 Tweezer pattern.

Exhibit 1.25 Bullish belt-hold tweezer.

Exhibit 1.26 Engulfing Bozu tweezer.

Exhibit 1.27 Hammer tweezer.

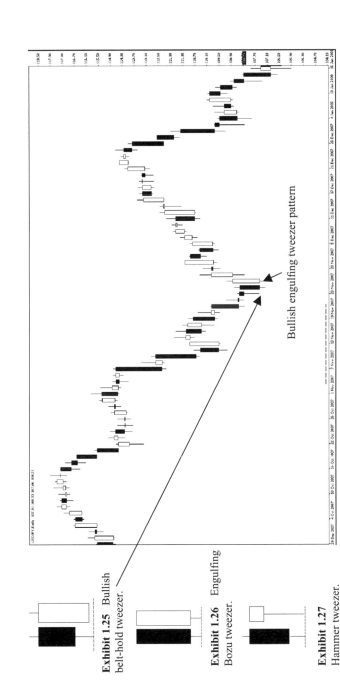

(source MetaQuotes Software Corp)

Figure 1.28 USD/JPY daily chart showing a bullish engulfing tweezer pattern.

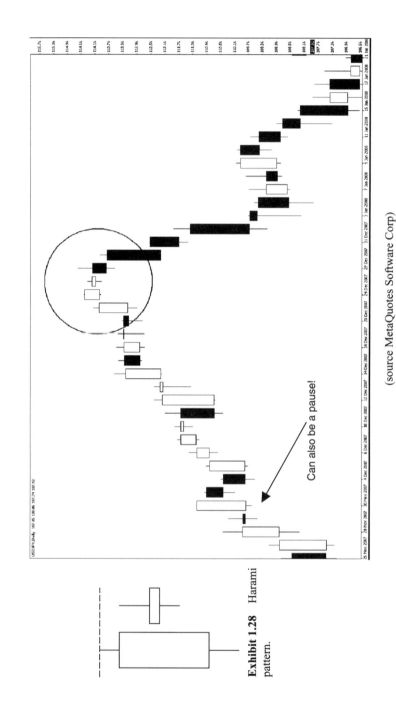

Exhibit 1.28 Harami pattern.

Figure 1.29 USD/JPY daily chart showing a classic harami signal after a rise in price action.
(source MetaQuotes Software Corp)

The Harami Bottom

This signal is found at turning points. It may, however, need a few sessions before it takes effect in the desired direction. It is the opposite of the engulfing pattern. Again, with most of these double candles the signals point to a threat to the previous market sentiment either as uncertainty or confirmation of support or resistance levels. The harami signal points out that there is uncertainty. A stronger version is the harami cross. The colour of both candles is not important, they can be the same. The body, however, must be contained within the previous session.

The Doji Evening Star

The final candlestick signal in this section is the doji evening star and doji morning star scenario. It is a popular set up amongst candlestick traders. This combination is a warning that the market sentiment has changed. The third candle is important and more significant if it becomes an engulfing candle as in the example in Figure 1.31 on page 45.

The Doji Morning Star

The opposite applies at support levels. As in Exhibit 1.31 on page 46 the third candle is an engulfing candle that places greater emphasis on the power of that signal. The importance of finding confirmation remains the same as for all candlestick signals but this particular scenario stands out quite well as a basing scenario.

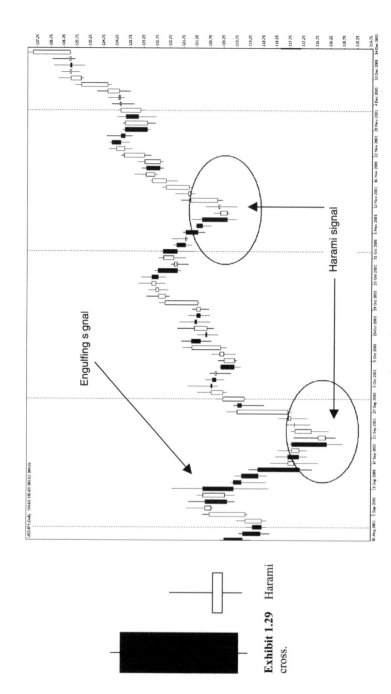

Exhibit 1.29 Harami cross.

Figure 1.30 USD/JPY weekly chart with two harami type signals. (source MetaQuotes Software Corp)

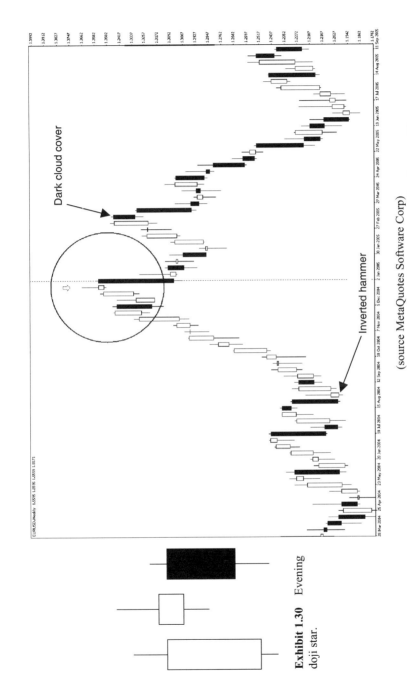

Exhibit 1.30 Evening doji star.

Figure 1.31 EUR/USD weekly chart with a good example of an engulfing pattern. (source MetaQuotes Software Corp)

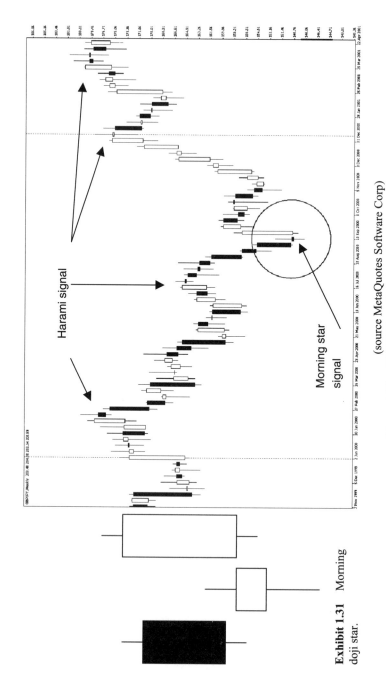

Exhibit 1.31 Morning doji star.

Figure 1.32 GBP/JPY weekly chart showing a morning star scenario.
(source MetaQuotes Software Corp)

Candlesticks = Signals 47

SOME CANDLESTICK EXAMPLES

- Bullish harami;
- Inverted hammer;
- Tweezer top;
- Bullish engulfing;
- Shooting star;
- Marabozu candlestick.

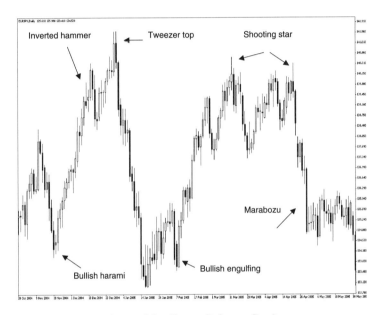

(source MetaQuotes Software Corp)

Figure 1.33 EUR/JPY daily chart showing candlestick examples.

SOME FURTHER CANDLESTICK EXAMPLES

- Bullish engulfing;
- Harami;
- Marabozu with mid-point resistance and later support level;
- Hammer.

(source MetaQuotes Software Corp)

Figure 1.34 USD/CAD daily chart with candlestick examples.

CHART ANALYSIS EXERCISE 1

Find the following candlestick signals on Figure 1.35:

- Doji (spinning tops);
- Bullish belt-hold line;
- Tweezer top;
- Bearish engulfing;
- Marabozu;
- Hanging man;
- Hammer;
- Bullish engulfing.

(source MetaQuotes Software Corp)

Figure 1.35 AUS/USD daily chart showing various candlestick types.

CHART ANALYSIS EXERCISE 1 – ANSWERS

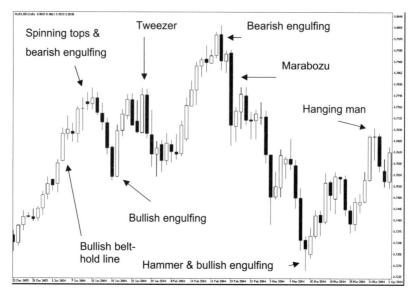

(source MetaQuotes Software Corp)

Figure 1.36 AUS/USD daily chart showing candlestick patterns.

SUMMARY

This chapter has outlined an abridged version of Japanese candlesticks and demonstrated that by applying these patterns it is possible to gain insight very quickly into a market that would otherwise be difficult to decipher. Weekly candlesticks charts and monthly candlesticks are more reliable than daily and hourly candlesticks, and it is vital, as discussed later in this book, that the bigger long-term market be applied to any daily charts. It is also important to ask yourself when looking at candlestick patterns the same question: "where is this candlestick?, is it in the context of other technical aspects that are at the same price level?"

Switching from weekly to daily candlesticks can help enormously in deciphering the market. For example, a weekly candlestick scenario, such as the hanging man in Figure 1.37 opposite, will help to confirm the daily chart technical picture. In this scenario the top of the hanging man on the weekly chart is a resistance level. A line taken from the top of the weekly hanging man and placed on the daily chart, as in Figure 1.38 opposite, demonstrates the resistance level at work. Spinning top candlestick types form during the early part of the trading week and suggest uncertainty in the market at that level.

Candlesticks = Signals   51

(source MetaQuotes Software Corp)

Figure 1.37 EUR/JPY weekly chart with a large hanging man candlestick finding support at the 10-week moving average.

(source MetaQuotes Software Corp)

Figure 1.38 EUR/JPY daily chart demonstrating the inner workings of the weekly hanging man.

Each attempt beyond the high of the hanging man candlestick level is clearly rejected on the daily chart. There are shadows or wicks above the candlesticks' real body that form at that level and which are clearly showing that the price action is finding selling pressure. Each of the spinning tops, likewise, never produced a daily close beyond that resistance level and eventually, as the market begins to move away, the daily candlesticks that appear over the following sessions produce lower highs. This is another very valuable clue that the market has come under selling pressure. Eventually, a harami type candlestick signals the decline in the EUR/JPY. Although a brief attempt higher results in a tweezer that might have shaken some investors out of their positions, the hanging man candle from the weekly chart proved to be a very powerful signal!

Japanese candlesticks provide clear market signals but they need to be placed in context and together with other techniques in order to confirm the candlestick signal. Candlesticks can give warning of change and sometimes imminent change in market direction.

Candlesticks are equally useful for showing areas of market support and resistance and are very good for creating pivot lines (pivot lines are discussed in Chapter 3). Candlesticks, however, can be complicated and at times lead to the wrong conclusion. For this reason it is always important to confirm the signal using other candles and other chart techniques. Try to keep the basic outline as discussed in this chapter when looking for candlestick signals and be patient when you find them. A bullish harami, for example, may take another one or two sessions before the signal begins to unfold. It may take you many years of practice to become fluent in their application, and there are many set ups and scenarios that require intensive study before basing an investment decision on candlesticks alone.

The signals that have been presented in this chapter should be seen as a visual representation of market sentiment and, as will be discussed later in this book, are used in ways that help to make a decision about market direction. Looking for signals should be a straightforward process. Always begin by looking at the high and the low and then the open and the close in order to determine the strength of market sentiment.

The open and the close helps to determine the main area of trading that has taken place as does the open and close in relation to the previous candle. The shadows, remember, are signs of selling pressure or buying pressure. A series of lower lows suggests weakness whereas a series of higher highs suggests strength.

In this chapter, candlesticks have been presented in a very basic manner in order to show how the process of monitoring the market can become easier when these signals stand out as visual clues about change in market sentiment that may present opportunities worth exploiting.

2
Chart Patterns = Opportunity

Chart patterns are found in all markets but some markets such as the Global Foreign Exchange markets have patterns that appear frequently as chart patterns re-occur in the financial markets. They may occasionally be difficult to see or difficult to interpret, but they are there and charting is simply a matter of recognising these patterns and incorporating them within a trading strategy. Head and shoulders and double tops/ double bottoms belong to some of the most popular and frequently seen chart patterns in the foreign exchange markets. There are some chart technicians who look for these patterns and variations of these patterns as they know that even if they themselves are not basing an investment decision on these patterns, many traders and investors around the world will be and that these patterns can therefore influence the markets accordingly.

That patterns re-occur reinforces the fact that market price action repeats itself. Patterns provide traders and investors with opportunity, and one unique advantage about patterns is that they can be used to measure for potential price targets. It is, however, the continuation of a trend that they are best suited as they not only confirm the conviction of market direction but also provide technical traders with the opportunity to join a trending market. A good rule to follow is for a continuation pattern to break out in the direction of the trend, that is to say, a continuation pattern will see price exit the pattern in the direction that the market entered the pattern.

The first part of this chapter covers those patterns that represent continuation in the current price trend. These are the most significant as they add confidence to your position or present a new opportunity to add to an existing position. The reversal patterns, although useful in finding a turning point in a market, can be complicated and take a long time to develop; these patterns are covered in the second part of this chapter.

CONTINUATION PATTERNS

- Bull flags;
- Pennants;
- Triangles;
- Wedges;
- Inverted head and shoulders.

REVERSAL PATTERNS

- Head and shoulders reversal;
- Triple tops/bottoms;
- Double tops/bottoms;
- "V" tops/bottoms;
- Broadening pattern.

BULL FLAGS

Flags are seen at the mid point of an advance in the market and are for the most part a short-term pattern usually taking between one and three weeks to develop, although this can vary. The bull flag begins to unfold after an advance in price action, usually a very steep advance, where the price advance is fast, leaving a distinctive series of nearly vertical price movements on the chart. The daily standard type candlestick that opens near the lows and closes near the highs, as shown in Figure 2.1 opposite, can be seen clearly during the forming of the flag pole. The chart, which has virtually no candlesticks that have shadows, is a sign that the market is confident. The flag forms when the price stops its advance and consolidates. The price action tends to decline but the two lines must contain the highs and lows in a slightly downward angle, creating a parallelogram that is slightly opposing the recent bullish activity.

BEAR FLAGS

This is the same as the bull flag but with bearish implications. The pattern is useful because it is possible to measure the flag pole and use it as a possible price objective upon a break out from the consolidation period. Confirmation is best with the flag pattern by watching for the flag to develop and then waiting for the break out to

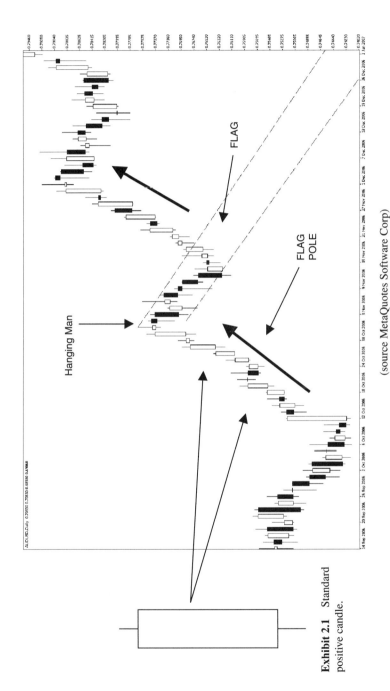

Exhibit 2.1 Standard positive candle.

Figure 2.1 AUS/USD daily chart with a bull flag pattern. The flag pole is used as a measuring technique with the "flag" flying at half mast.

(source MetaQuotes Software Corp)

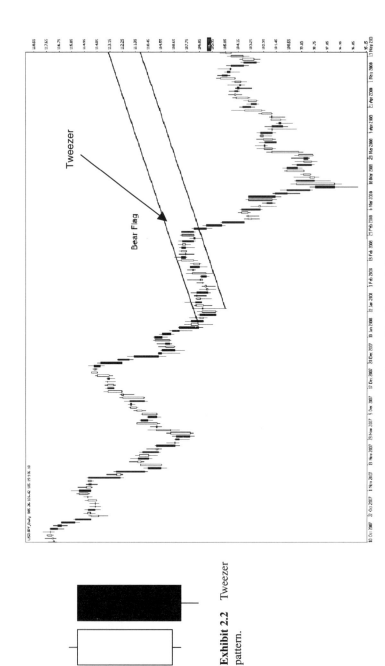

Figure 2.2 USD/JPY daily chart with a bear flag scenario with price action consolidating between two parallel lines.
(source MetaQuotes Software Corp)

Exhibit 2.2 Tweezer pattern.

Chart Patterns = Opportunity

occur before looking to enter or add to positions. It is a similar situation to the bull flag except that the market may tend to break out faster in a down trend. The pattern remains the same as with the bull flag, only the opposite. The bear flag is sloping slightly higher against the trend and the break out is in the same direction that the price entered the flag.

BULL PENNANT

This pattern is similar to the flag in that it forms within the same amount of time that it takes to form a flag. It is different in the shape and tends to be within converging lines rather than parallel lines. As with the flag the pole is used as a measuring technique. Wait for a break out to occur in order to confirm the pattern.

The price action should not reach the apex during the formation of the pennant type pattern and the price should not move back too far in the direction of the trend. That is to say, in the direction of the mast that has formed during the fast price movement.

BEAR PENNANT

The same applies to a bearish pennant where the price forms between converging lines rather than parallel lines. The price should conclude the pattern before reaching the apex with a characteristic sharp break out where prices then continue in the direction of the trend. The trend is also an important characteristic of the pennant in as much as the market is usually trending faster than normal, characterised by large standard type candlesticks.

BULL SYMMETRICAL TRIANGLE

This pattern signal has at least five points of contact within the converging lines. The price breaks out before the apex is reached. As a rough guide the break out occurs two-thirds of the way into the pattern but this will vary according to market conditions and in extreme circumstances the price can return to the apex.

BEAR SYMMETRICAL TRIANGLE

Ascending Triangle

This pattern is similar to the symmetrical triangle pattern in that it breaks out approximately two-thirds of the way into the pattern but this can vary according to market conditions. The pattern differs, however, in form. In an upwards trend the upper line is horizontal and the lower line is sloping upwards. The pattern can sometimes appear like a bottoming pattern. The market breaks out and closes over the horizontal line.

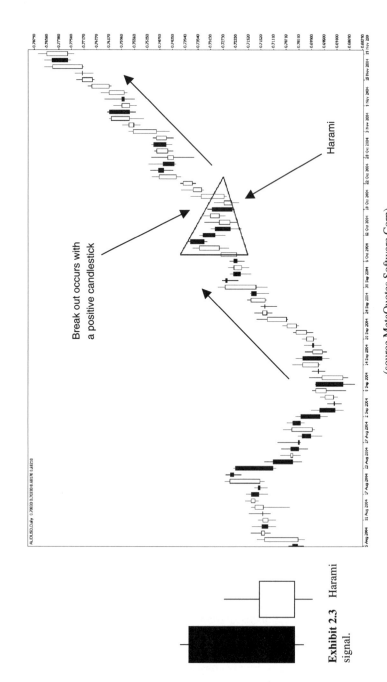

Figure 2.3 AUS/USD daily chart with a bullish pennant that is not unlike the flag pattern.
(source MetaQuotes Software Corp)

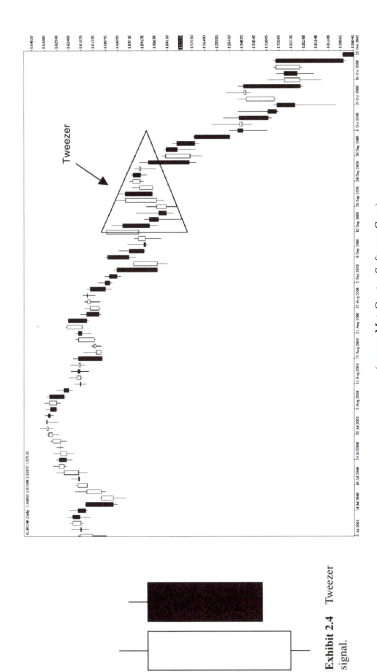

Figure 2.4 EUR/CHF daily chart showing a bearish pennant that is not unlike the bear flag pattern. (source MetaQuotes Software Corp)

Exhibit 2.4 Tweezer signal.

(source MetaQuotes Software Corp)

Figure 2.5 Gold daily chart showing a bullish symmetrical triangle as part of an upwards trend market. Price breaks out before apex.

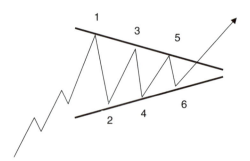

Exhibit 2.5 Bullish symmetrical triangle.

Chart Patterns = Opportunity

(source MetaQuotes Software Corp)

Figure 2.6 USD/CHF daily chart with bearish symmetrical triangle.

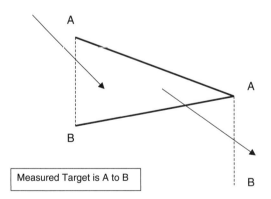

Exhibit 2.6 Bearish symmetrical triangle.

(source MetaQuotes Software Corp)

Figure 2.7 EUR/GBP daily chart showing a ascending triangle.

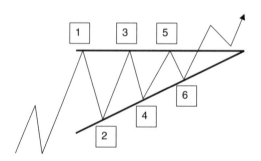

Exhibit 2.7 Ascending triangle.

Chart Patterns = Opportunity

(source MetaQuotes Software Corp)

Figure 2.8   USD/CHF daily chart showing a descending triangle.

Descending Triangle

The descending triangle is seen as being a bearish continuation pattern. A feature of this pattern is the strong selling that takes place on moves to the upside creating lower highs. Watching for certain bearish candlestick patterns to form at these levels is useful. A break out below the flat lower line followed by a return move at some point to the lower line confirms resistance.

BULL FALLING WEDGE

The bull market falling wedge is similar to the symmetrical triangle. The difference is that both lines slope away from the trend. As with the triangle this pattern breaks approximately two-thirds of the way into the pattern but can vary. In a down trend the bearish wedge tends to form quicker than the bullish wedge. Figure 2.9 overleaf demonstrates how a bull market falling wedge can form on a chart.

(source MetaQuotes Software Corp)

Figure 2.9 AUS/USD daily chart with a falling wedge.

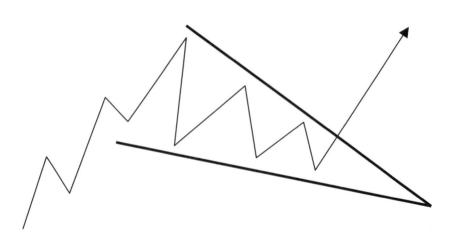

Exhibit 2.8 Bullish falling wedge.

BEAR RISING WEDGE

This follows the same principles as the bull market falling wedge except that the bear market rising wedge should be sloping upwards. The wedge signifies continuation and that is how these patterns should be applied to charts unless proven otherwise. The market will move in the path of least resistance. Again, expect the break out in the direction of the entry.

(source MetaQuotes Software Corp)

Figure 2.10 USD/JPY daily chart showing a bear market rising wedge where the price enters and exits in the same direction.

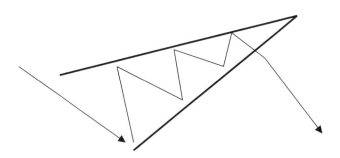

Exhibit 2.9 Bearish rising wedge.

INVERTED HEAD AND SHOULDERS CONTINUATION

The inverted head and shoulders has the same features as the reversal pattern but the inverted head and shoulders pattern is always in the direction of the trend.

(source MetaQuotes Software Corp)

Figure 2.11 GBP/USD daily chart with inverted head and shoulders.

(source MetaQuotes Software Corp)

Figure 2.12 GBP/USD daily chart showing a channel and head and shoulders.

PART TWO – REVERSAL PATTERNS

Reversal patterns are different to continuation patterns in that they can take much longer to complete, leading to choppy market conditions during the formation period. A reversal pattern must appear after a trending market, preferably after a long period of trending either up or down, otherwise the pattern may simply not produce the expected reversal in price action. The application of trend lines, as discussed in the following chapter, should be applied to any type of trend in order to find the break of the trend. Breaking the line is not always a precursor to a reversal but simply suggests that the trend line is no longer valid, at which point a reversal pattern could begin to develop.

Patterns are common in all markets but some patterns are more frequent than others. A well-known pattern is the head and shoulders reversal pattern which is identified most often in all markets. A pattern known as a diamond, however, as the name suggests, is not so frequent.

BULLISH HEAD AND SHOULDERS REVERSAL PATTERN

This pattern is probably the most widely known amongst traders and investors. The pattern forms after a trend. Normally, a distinctive feature is the three attempts to move higher, with the middle peak the highest. There is a return move to the neckline which should hold the price action back (be concerned if it does not and check that the pivot is drawn correctly). This pattern can sometimes be complex but is therefore more effective.

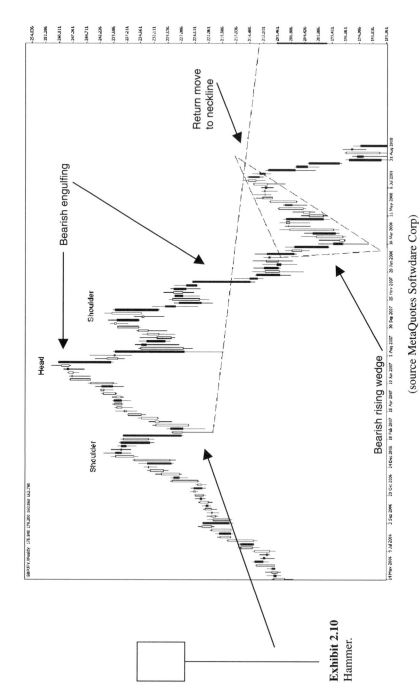

Figure 2.13 GBP/JPY daily chart with a head and shoulders pattern. Observing two daily closes below the neckline helps to confirm the neckline. (source MetaQuotes Softwdare Corp)

Chart Patterns = Opportunity

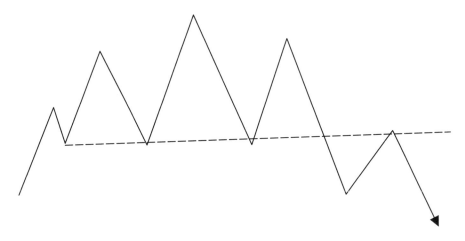

Exhibit 2.11 Head and shoulders.

BEARISH HEAD AND SHOULDERS REVERSAL PATTERN

The left shoulder is the continuation of the trend with the head being lower than the left shoulder but the right shoulder not as low as the head. Measuring the distance between the peak of the head and the neckline creates a potential measured target. The best way to determine this is to find this pattern on charts and try out the measuring technique. Look to see how the market reacts at the neckline, that is to say, look for closes above or below the neckline in order to help confirm the level and then see how the market reacts once the target has been reached.

TRIPLE TOP PATTERN

The triple top/bottom pattern signal (sometimes known as the "W" or "M" pattern), is not as frequent as the double top/bottom pattern but is traded in the same way. A break out occurs which can be useful as a market entry point. The triple top is more or less the same as a head and shoulders pattern. The centre peak is not as prominent, ending parallel with the first peak.

TRIPLE BOTTOM PATTERN

This pattern is simply the opposite of the triple top. There is no difference and as with triple tops and double tops and bottoms, the pattern is not always as well defined, as shown in the chart example.

(source MetaQuotes Software Corp)

Figure 2.14 AUD/CAD daily chart with a head and shoulders bottom.

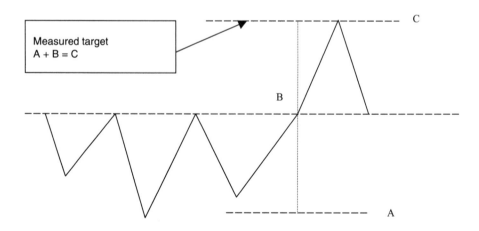

Exhibit 2.12 Head and shoulders bottom.

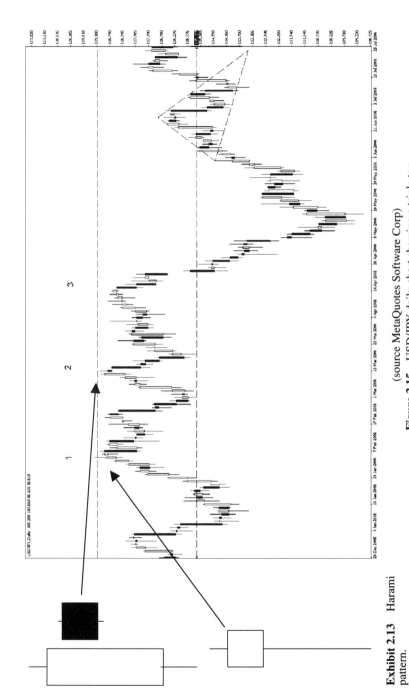

Exhibit 2.13 Harami pattern.

(source MetaQuotes Software Corp)
Figure 2.15 USD/JPY daily chart showing a triple top.

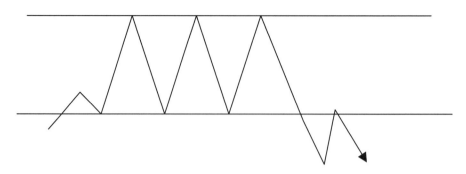

Exhibit 2.14 Hanging man.

THE DOUBLE TOP PATTERN

This pattern is found frequently in the markets and is probably one of the best known and used signals. The double top pattern appears when the market makes a second attempt to move higher, usually after the trend line has been broken. This pattern is seen very often in the foreign exchange markets and not only on daily charts. As with the triple top/bottom there is eventually a break away which, like the head and shoulders pattern, has a price objective and a return move to the neckline.

THE DOUBLE BOTTOM PATTERN

This follows the same principles as the double top. The pattern is not always as straightforward as in the example in Figure 2.18 on page 75. A reaction occurs during the second test of the low, resulting in buying activity. The second low, as in Exhibit 2.18 on page 76, may not reach the same level as the first low. A price objective is found by taking the highest point between the two reaction lows and projecting this upward, as with the triple top and bottom and head and shoulders pattern.

THE BULLISH AND BEARISH "V" PATTERN

This type of pattern, also referred to as a "Spike", happens quite quickly which causes distress in the market and tends to be difficult to see until it has formed. The result of the fast buying or selling sees a rapid reaction in that the market goes back the other way just as quickly.

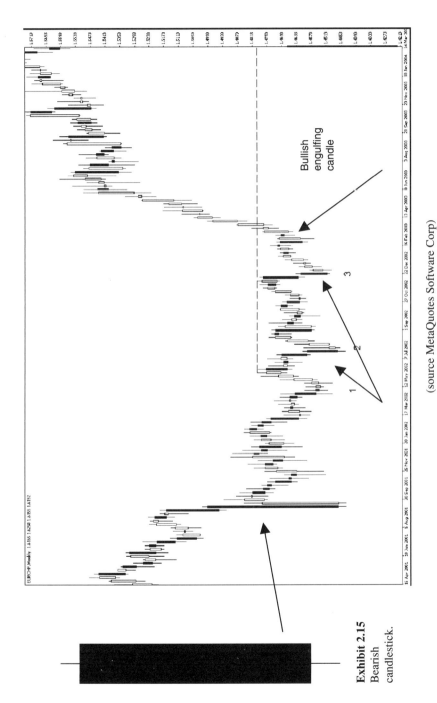

Figure 2.16 USD/JPY daily chart showing a triple bottom.
(source MetaQuotes Software Corp)

Exhibit 2.15 Bearish candlestick.

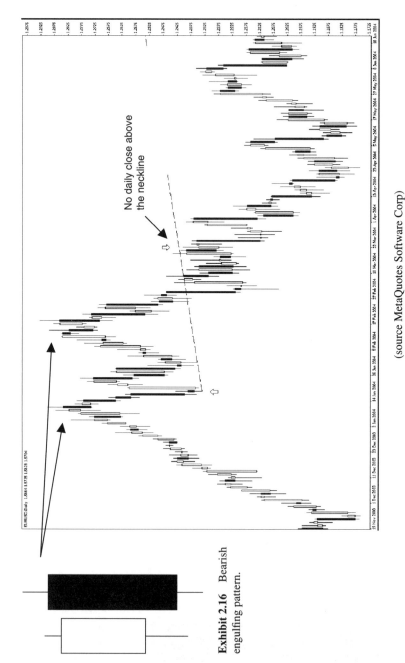

Exhibit 2.16 Bearish engulfing pattern.

(source MetaQuotes Software Corp)
Figure 2.17 EUR/USD daily chart showing a double top pattern.

Chart Patterns = Opportunity 75

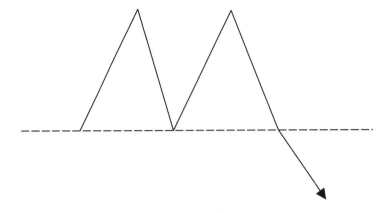

Exhibit 2.17 Double top scenario.

(source MetaQuotes Software Corp)

Figure 2.18 AUS/USD daily chart showing a double bottom pattern with measured target.

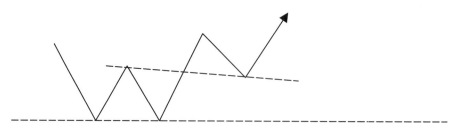

Exhibit 2.18 Double bottom scenario.

A noticeable difference between spike tops and spike bottoms, looking at them close up on the weekly chart in Figure 2.19, is the market at the top which, while still producing higher highs, the real body of the positive candles are quite small.

However, the negative candles are very large and distinct in comparison, suggesting faster moves to the downside that caused a great deal of distress within that market. This is a good example of why tops are usually quicker to form and more volatile than bottoms.

(source MetaQuotes Software Corp)

Figure 2.19 USD/JPY weekly chart with a "V" type pattern.

BULLISH "V" TOP

The small white candles suggest a less than positive market that is moving up very slowly implying hope! Where there is hope there is danger. Typically, this type of market becomes volatile upon the release of some news or central bank statement, forcing the market into confusion and running stop orders in the process.

BEARISH "V" BOTTOM

The market at the bottom of the spike displays a very balanced market.

Standard negative candles leading down to a hammer day and eventually standard positive candles lead the way back up. This type of market condition is more suitable for entering a position with less chance of the market experiencing wild swings that take out the stop loss orders. In Figure 2.21 on page 79, the recent downward trend has culminated in candlestick types that have long shadows, suggesting that the price has been feeling the market and has found support. The overall conditions are much less volatile than at the market top.

THE BROADENING TOP AND BOTTOM

The broadening pattern occurs over a long period of time on daily charts. The pattern has five to six points of contact with the trend lines and on or after that there is usually a failed attempt to reach the line where the market conviction for a turn finally begins to unfold. This pattern occurs mostly after an extensive bull market. Traders and investors experience whipsaw type market conditions. Some technicians believe that the pattern is most commonly found at market tops and less at market bottoms because this is a pattern that is caused by many market participants that are caught up after an extensive bull market.

Although it is difficult for long-term traders to find suitable entry for positions, the lower line can be seen as a base line enabling positions to be placed at this level once the line has been validated by watching for at least two daily closes above the lower line and at a later point after the five or six points have been established at which to watch for a failed return to the lower line. This type of pattern usually represents mass confusion on a grand scale and corresponding whipsaw market conditions. The broadening pattern usually occurs at the end of a bull or bear market.

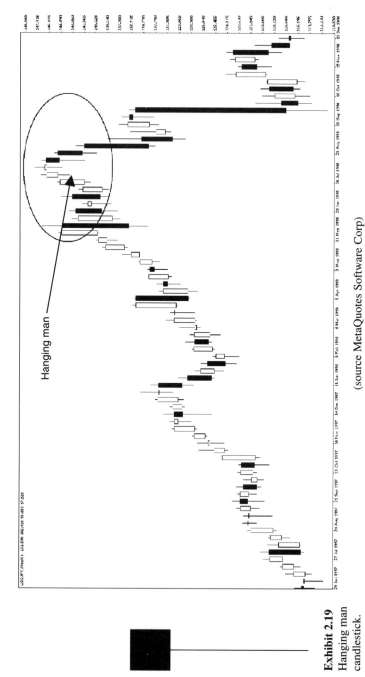

Exhibit 2.19
Hanging man candlestick.

(source MetaQuotes Software Corp)
Figure 2.20 USD/JPY daily chart showing a "V" top pattern.

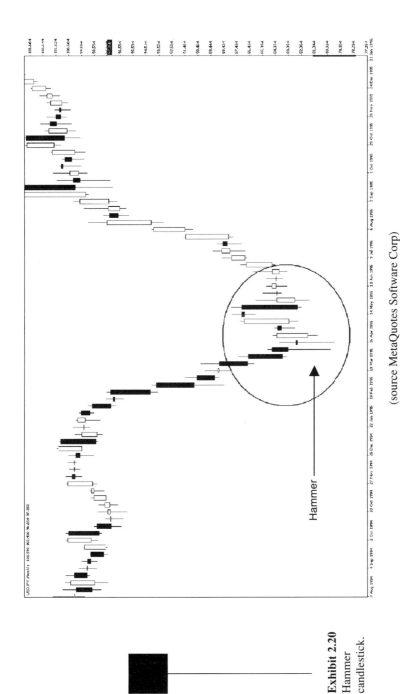

Figure 2.21 USD/JPY weekly chart with negative candles and positive candles are more or less balanced, a sign of equilibrium in the market.

(source MetaQuotes Software Corp)

Exhibit 2.20 Hammer candlestick.

(source MetaQuotes Software Corp)

Figure 2.22 EUR/GBP daily chart with a large bullish broadening pattern. This pattern usually has five or six points of contact before moving out of the pattern.

(source MetaQuotes Software Corp)

Figure 2.23 USD/CAD daily chart with a large broadening bottom.

Chart Patterns = Opportunity 81

(source MetaQuotes Software Corp)

Figure 2.24 EUR/CHF weekly chart showing pattern examples.

SOME CHART PATTERN EXAMPLES

- Large double top pattern with a measured target at approximately where the broadening pattern is seen;
- Two bearish flags;
- A broadening pattern.

CHART ANALYSIS EXERCISE 2

Find the following patterns and candles in Figure 2.25:

- Bullish rising wedge;
- Double top;
- Bear flag.

(source MetaQuotes Software Corp)

Figure 2.25 EUR/USD daily chart with patterns.

Chart Patterns = Opportunity

CHART ANALYSIS EXERCISE 2 – ANSWERS

(source MetaQuotes Software Corp)

Figure 2.26 EUR/USD daily chart with patterns.

SUMMARY

In this chapter chart patterns have been discussed and it has been shown that they produce opportunities for the technical trader. It is important to remember that while some model text book patterns in form and shape, some do not, and can seem almost inefficient with no definite distinguishable shape to work from until after the break out occurs.

Once the break out occurs it is the technical trader's responsibility to find and attempt to verify the break out and any potential targets that should be seen and incorporated within a trading strategy. When a break out occurs it should be applied on a discretionary basis, but should be part of a strategy. Waiting for a break out to occur based on research of previous break outs may result in a missed opportunity or even a false break out being traded with little progress. Trading and investing is not an exact science therefore being prepared for an event should be adequate enough rather than having a fixed expectation that a market break out will occur just because the pattern is 75 % complete!

Studying patterns and back testing them to find confirmation is really not essential to trading and investing. The reason for this is that, if you back test a bullish falling wedge and find that the market breaks out between 71 % and 75 % of the way to the apex you might find that the one time you see a perfect looking pattern it breaks out sooner than anticipated, creating a missed opportunity because the expectation was that the pattern still had a few more sessions to go before the break out would occur.

Continuation patterns carry greater importance than reversal patterns; they are also easier to trade than reversal patterns as reversal patterns can take a long time to form and are often volatile during the formation period. The continuation pattern is important because it signals a pause in a trending market. A good continuation pattern has the characteristics of an uncertain market. This is because the market is consolidating and as many of the continuation patterns in this chapter have demonstrated, there is a move slightly against the prior major trend.

The reason that a good trend consolidates is that a trend needs bouts of profit taking otherwise all the trades will be one way and the market becomes stale. A market that has congested price action and is rising very slowly in an up trend is not a good sign; it implies hope on behalf of the market participants.

Continuation patterns also give traders and investors that have bad positions in the market an opportunity to square up their positions. Both new positions and squaring up bad positions for a small profit or loss go to forming these patterns. The average continuation pattern therefore lasts between five and 20 working days. Any more than this and things might not work out simply because a trending market will not hang about, it will move! Continuation patterns therefore provide traders and investors with an opportunity to join the trend and a trending environment is where traders and investors make the majority of their money. A very important feature of a trending market is that the trend is relatively calm, which can also be a little disconcerting.

There are more patterns than are covered in this book and it is recommended that an in-depth study of chart patterns be pursued. It should also be remembered that not all patterns will be 100 % reliable and can often break out in a false direction.

The point of this chapter, however, is to clarify those patterns that are observed most frequently in the Forex markets and that have a very definite break out signal when the break out occurs. That is to say, the use of candlesticks works well with these patterns. Above all, patterns provide great opportunities for technical traders and investors. However, as with the chapter on Japanese candlesticks, the objective is to become familiar with patterns and then incorporate them within a strategy and trade them discretionally, rather than looking for some other pattern or candlestick signal to appear for reassurance, it might then be too late!

3
Buying and Selling = Support and Resistance Levels

In Chapters 1 and 2, evidence has been presented that endorses the fact that a chart is a useful method of identifying opportunity by observing chart signals that display signs of a possible change in market sentiment. These signals are found over and over again regardless of what the economic or fundamental situation is and regardless of how irrational the markets become. These signals allow the technical trader to observe and monitor the price action of the markets with relative ease once they have become familiar.

The candlestick signals discussed in Chapter 1 demonstrate clearly that it is possible to find investment opportunities based on the type of candlestick signal that is produced after a daily or weekly session. Forming at certain levels, these signals yield clues about market sentiment.

Chapter 2 demonstrated that it is also possible to find markets that are trending, consolidating before continuing or reversing altogether. These patterns allow the technical trader to monitor continuation or reversal and create potential targets.

This chapter aims to compliment the two previous chapters by showing how to create a context in which the developing price action becomes more apparent, thus making the signals stronger when seen in relation to an area of support or resistance, by considering that the financial markets are either moving upwards, sideways or downwards. These are the three possibilities, there are no more.

The following themes are covered in this chapter:

- support and resistance levels;
- trend lines;
- intermediate trend lines;
- pivot lines;
- Fibonacci levels.

The following techniques will help you as a technical trader to identify, confirm and monitor a market that is trending, consolidating or reversing. The techniques will also identify areas where market *stop orders* can be positioned. In some instances these same techniques can also produce possible price objectives. The techniques and methods used for finding support and resistance on charts are very simple yet very effective, applications that modify the chart until it becomes a transparent picture of the real market situation at hand.

If all fundamental and economic news is known and discounted by the price action at these areas of support or resistance and the market then begins to turn that is a warning that market participants, especially technical traders, have absorbed the news and fundamental statements and any other number of reasons and are now buying or selling on the market for a reason.

This is why the chart that displays a bearish or bullish signal is clearly an advantage to any technical trader, regardless of what the fundamental and economical reasons are. But finding resistance or support levels beforehand that are possibly going to have a very significant impact on the price allows the technical trader to prepare for a change in market sentiment even before such bullish or bearish signals appear. Combining predetermined levels with signals gives the technical trader an edge. It also buys time to change or modify an existing plan or strategy and adopt a more cautious stance. This type of practice will also make signals much clearer to interpret when they appear in context of an important level that is already determined and positioned on the chart.

When a change of direction in the market begins to unfold it is often accompanied by news related reasons or some fundamental factor as investors look for reasons to explain the change in sentiment. In some forex markets, economic releases can be followed as investors and traders panic and exit their positions creating volatile conditions in the process and pointing to the economic release as the cause. If a technical trader has reason to believe that technically a price level on the chart is strong enough to maintain resistance or support, this predetermined level will help maintain confidence during such market shake outs.

SUPPORT AND RESISTANCE

A market that is trending upwards is trending higher by making higher highs and higher lows on the chart (lower lows and lower highs in a downwards trend). The market must be clearing resistance levels, previous highs, pivot lines, intermediate trend lines and holding at support levels during corrections in order for it to remain intact. The first sign of a market penetrating support (resistance in a downtrend), might signal a change in direction.

There are days where the market will push lower (or higher) through previous lows (highs) and then return to its trending environment, but this is quite often an economic news-related incident such as Non Farm Payrolls released on the first

Buying and Selling = Support and Resistance Levels

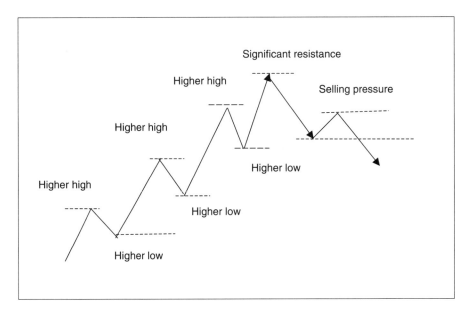

Exhibit 3.1 Series of higher highs and higher lows.

(source MetaQuotes Software Corp)

Figure 3.1 EUR/GBP daily chart showing price action making higher highs and higher lows.

(source MetaQuotes Software Corp)

Figure 3.2 USD/CAD weekly chart showing support levels and resistance levels. Old support becomes resistance and resistance becomes support.

Friday of the month. Such incidents are best avoided and most short-term professionals will cut back their positions on such days to avoid being caught badly in the market.

Japanese candlesticks are actually very useful for measuring the trending activity in a market by observing the higher highs and higher lows, and visa versa. Observing the market price action at important levels is analysing the current state of market sentiment. A filter of a daily close or two daily closes above or below a level is useful in order to confirm a break out of a pattern or a break above or below an important support or resistance level. However, once the price action pushes through an area of resistance or below an area of support, the level ceases to be resistance and then becomes support; this is often called the principle of polarity. The importance given to these levels often depends on the time frame of the investment as a trending market has more importance for a long term based position than a range bound market. If a market is range bound, the market may react at a resistance level for many weeks or even months before that level is broken. The polarity level may become a time line as many short-term traders sell or buy against such levels with little or no concern for the overall bullish or bearish sentiment of the market.

Buying and Selling = Support and Resistance Levels 89

(source MetaQuotes Software Corp)

Figure 3.3 GBP/USD daily chart showing resistance and support levels, resistance becomes support and support becomes resistance, the principle of polarity.

Any market makes highs and lows and does so because of buying and selling. Figure 3.2 on page 88 demonstrates this quite well. The weekly chart shows that as the market broke below previous support more selling would have taken place. When the market turns upwards towards the old support (now resistance), more selling activity happened again. Traders that entered short positions in the market will have sold again and longs that entered the market and were wrong will have wanted to get out and therefore selling their position back again created more selling activity. These are areas where there is buying pressure; they are seen as support on the chart. During a downtrend phase of market action, the area where selling pressure is greater than buying pressure is known as resistance.

For a technical trader to confirm or attempt to forecast future levels of support requires that one first finds the potential levels of resistance. The weekly candlestick charts in Figures 3.2 and 3.3 demonstrate this process quite well. A previous area of resistance becomes an area of support (polarity). Visually, these areas are created by simply placing lines from old support and resistance areas and observing the market at these levels, especially the candlestick type.

TREND LINES

An equally well-used method is to apply a trend line and follow the price action in relation to the line. A reaction to the line can confirm the trend. A break in that trend line can demonstrate uncertainty or weakness. There are three time horizons normally associated with trends.

Short term: From minutes to days. This time frame is typically a market maker's view and can be as short as a few minutes and hours. A position trader will see short term as being anything from one day up to two weeks.

Medium term: From days and weeks to months. This time period is mostly linked to short-term investments and option traders who might typically look for a period of weeks up to three months as their time horizon.

Long term: Anything from six months to 10 years. Fund Managers look to this time period but incorporate and apply short-term trends in order to optimise positions.

1. Basic concept – a trend in motion will remain in motion. Market price action moves in the path of least resistance; a trend line can show that the market price action is moving in the direction of least resistance.
2. The more reactions there are to a trend line the more significant it becomes as a line of confirmation.
3. A break in a trend line can warn of an imminent change in market sentiment.
4. Trend lines help the technical trader to find suitable price levels in order to place positions in the market.
5. The longer the trend line is in existence the more important it becomes. A trend line that appears on a chart for three years is more important than a trend line that has only been on the chart for six months.

A trend line demonstrating support in an up trend is drawn from left to right and should have at least two points of contact, that is, two reaction lows with the second reaction low being higher than the first. The price action corrects and finds support and then continues in the direction of the trend. The opposite applies in a down trend.

TREND LINE CHANNELS

Channels are established on charts by drawing a line parallel to the trend line. This should be drawn easily with the objective of containing the price action within the channel as much as possible. A good rule to follow when doing this is to have the two main points of contact that establish the primary trend line and then to look for

Buying and Selling = Support and Resistance Levels

(source MetaQuotes Software Corp)

Figure 3.4 GBP/JPY daily chart showing a long-term down trend and long-term up trend.

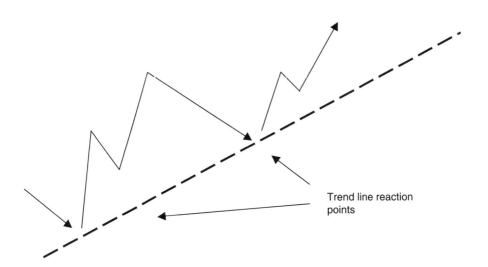

Exhibit 3.2 Trend line support.

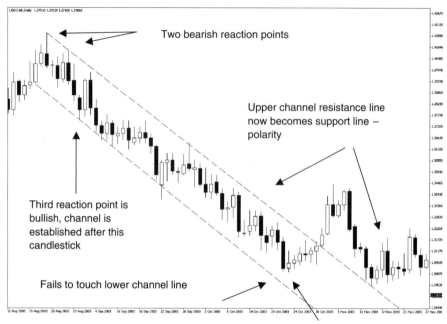

(source MetaQuotes Software Corp)

Figure 3.5 USD/CAD daily chart showing a good trend channel. The price action eventually fails to touch the lower trend line and a bullish harami candlestick appears.

the third point of contact at the opposite side parallel to the primary line in order to establish the channel. The parallel trend line will only change if there is a lower low than the previously established reaction point, but the channel should be established properly before the break out! Once the channel is established it represents not only the market sentiment, but also confirms that the market is moving in the path of least resistance, lower lows and lower highs, etc. In Figure 3.5, the market continues in the direction of the prevailing market sentiment until the market sentiment changes and prices break out of the channel, usually in the opposite direction.

Channels are not only useful for establishing the direction of the market, but also for finding the areas where the market sentiment may begin to change, that is to say, major support or resistance areas are being violated. For example, if prices have been moving down within a channel the price will have a series of reaction lows at the lower trend line, and a series of reaction highs at the parallel line. Watching for the point where the market fails to touch the lower line in a downtrend (the opposite in an upwards trend) can be useful and provide an early indication of a change in market sentiment.

Buying and Selling = Support and Resistance Levels

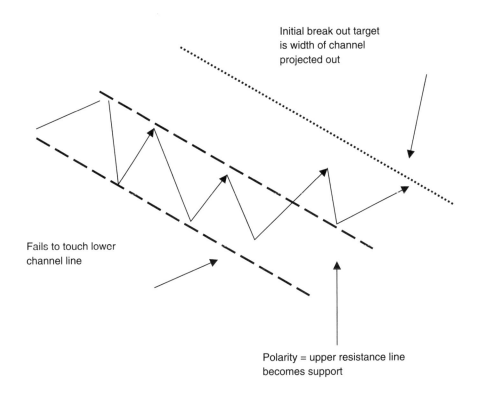

Exhibit 3.3 Channel principle.

Channels also provide technical traders with a potential targets. This is done by measuring the width of the channel and then projecting this width out in the direction of the break.

Long-term trend lines and channels are just as good for establishing the overall direction. This type of trend line channel helps long-term investors to remain with their positions. It also produces the most suitable area for maintaining stop orders in the market by establishing the parallel line as the point where the market is likely to falter, at that point the market stop order is likely to get hit.

A useful visual aspect of a bull market towards the end of a trend is the angle of the trend itself. A bull market will always be at its steepest angle and the steeper the gradient the more likely it is for the price to first break the trend line and then return to a more normal gradient before a complete reversal takes place. This is unique and visually very important to the technical trader. In a bull market there is often accompanying positive news and an optimistic feeling surrounding the market. The end of bull markets tends to be quite volatile as price action tries to consolidate with

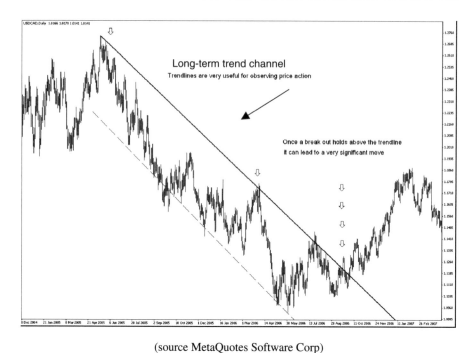

(source MetaQuotes Software Corp)

Figure 3.6 USD/CAD daily chart showing a long-term primary trend line and trend channel.

(source MetaQuotes Software Corp)

Figure 3.7 USD/JPY daily chart showing the break of a trend line suggesting that buyers are no longer supporting the price.

little or no fresh buying. Late traders and investors who have forgotten that a market might have been rallying for months or years can easily be frightened into getting out again as they entered at bad levels. This leads to confusion and distress. For this reason topping patterns are more violent than those patterns at the end of a bear market. Likewise, the break of a trend line can be an early clue to a change in market direction simply because there is no support. The initial change in a rallying market often occurs after a sudden increase in the angle of the trend.

INTERMEDIATE TREND LINES

The major and minor trend line is very good for finding break out points that occur in the trending market, and which are areas of continual support with intermediate pauses in the trend until resistance is finally overcome.

An intermediate trend line is produced at shorter periods of resistance (support) and confirms the importance of the level as an area where a break out will occur. Applying intermediate trend lines to candlestick charts can make it possible to establish the line at the level where the market is finding frequent selling or buying pressure, but not the strongest selling or buying pressure. The intermediate trend line established on candlesticks is drawn from the first two reaction highs or lows and then observed as the price action approaches the line. First attempts to clear the level should be treated with caution. Corresponding candlesticks will form at the intermediate line producing evidence of the market reaction to the level. However, until the level is clearly broken a false break cannot be ruled out and may occur, at which point a bearish candlestick beyond the intermediate level will have greater emphasis.

(source MetaQuotes Software Corp)

Figure 3.8 GBP/USD daily chart with a primary trend line and intermediate trend lines.

Clearly, many technical traders would draw their intermediate trend line along the peaks, especially on a bar chart. Here candlesticks display the market sentiment at such levels, indicating what the reaction might be found. This is clearly an advantage in using candlestick patterns.

Close inspection of the chart in Figure 3.10 on page 98 demonstrates the advantage of drawing such a trend line as it verifies the candlestick at such levels. The level is already established so when a bearish harami forms just above the level it can be a warning that the break out is a false break out. In Figure 3.10, the market paused at the line, then broke above it only to find selling pressure. The initial strategy at such a level would be to remain neutral if you were following the trend or even bearish for the short-term trade and to have a short position in the market just below the intermediate trend line.

Applying candlesticks to the chart and observing the reaction at certain levels provides you with an insider's view of the market sentiment, something bar charts cannot achieve.

INTERNAL TREND LINES

Internal trend lines are very useful when placed within an area where the price has been consolidating but where there is no distinguishable pattern. With this type of trend line it is not necessary to find a series of reaction highs or lows but instead the internal trend line is established where there are two or more reaction highs or lows at the beginning of the trend line similar to the primary trend line criteria. This type of trend line is drawn within an area where the market seems to be developing a pattern or looks set to react to a signal and can be situated along the top or bottom of a series of reactions. The more reactions there are the more conclusive the line becomes so that there is no question about its positioning. These lines are difficult to get right and are often seen only after they could have been most useful.

PIVOT LINES

As has just been demonstrated, there are trend lines that can be applied to the long-term trend and then reapplied as you filter down the charts to the short term and which allow the technical trader to analyse and determine the strength of the trend. In those areas where a market has tested a line the line becomes more conclusive until a decisive break out occurs and the market changes direction. Break outs can be filtered with a percentage close above or below the line, or two or three consecutive closes to validate the break out.

The pivot line, although similar to the intermediate support and resistance lines, has a value of its own. Pivot lines occur only at specific levels. For the most part they are predetermined levels and, unlike trend lines and intermediate trend lines which

Exhibit 3.4
Harami Candlestick Signal = Sell and proves to be a false break out.

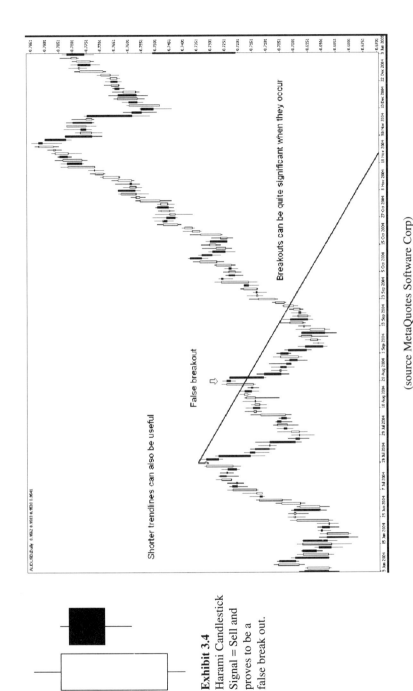

Figure 3.9 AUS/USD daily chart and an intermediate trend line and a false break. (source MetaQuotes Software Corp)

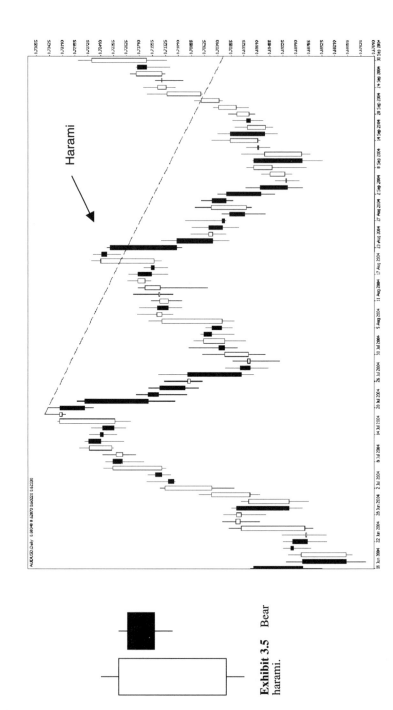

Figure 3.10 AUS/USD daily chart showing the false break out and a bearish harami pattern. (source MetaQuotes Software Corp)

Exhibit 3.5 Bear harami.

Buying and Selling = Support and Resistance Levels

(source MetaQuotes Software Corp)

Figure 3.11 EUR/CHF weekly chart demonstrating the use of an internal trend line that is at first support and then finally resistance.

are placed on the chart after the market has a reaction at two or more points, pivot lines are placed at areas where the price has one market reaction, either a reaction high or a reaction low. That said, they can also be determined by time and by calculation.

The most useful predetermined pivot lines are found at:

- the point where the market has a rejection and moves away fast, especially after a trending period. This is a key day pivot line;
- a daily high or low, such as a belt-hold line, closing bozu, engulfing pattern and marabozu candlestick;
- the high and low of the first trading day of the month;
- the high and low of the first hour of the first trading day of the week.

Pivot lines can help confirm market direction (this is their main application in this book), they are support and resistance like trend lines. It is, however, a level that, like the intermediate trend line, acts as short-term support or resistance, but where the price is more likely to rotate around the line until a direction is conclusive. The pivot is useful to the technical trader for observing price action during short-term

(source MetaQuotes Software Corp)

Figure 3.12 AUS/USD daily chart demonstrating resistance broken and later becoming support with a pivot lines at the top of a shooting star candlestick reaction high.

directional changes to the market. Its technical value is extremely helpful in deciding where to buy or sell on the market.

Figure 3.12 demonstrates quite well the difference between an intermediate trend line and a pivot line. The difficulty in using a reaction high or low is finding the right price level to position a valid line. A good general rule to follow when placing a reaction at the high or low pivot line is to study the candlestick type. A classic shooting star or hammer candle is useful for this purpose because both of these candlestick types, although signalling strong resistance or support, can and do signal continuation in the price direction. Therefore positioning a pivot line at the high or low of such candles and observing the price action to see if it reacts to the level can be useful for determining whether there is still conviction in the current direction. The price action might return to the line and rotate at that level until the market either continues or changes direction. The more the price action clusters and rotates at such levels the more significance the pivot line has.

Exhibit 3.6 opposite shows how a pivot line might be applied. Japanese candlesticks are very suitable for finding pivot lines and by watching candlesticks with significant shadows, such as the shooting star candlestick, they can be readily applied. The long shadow that demonstrates where the market has come under pressure is a warning, but having the pivot line on the chart for future reference is useful because if the market looks like it is going to continue then the pivot line will become the target for the price action.

Positioning pivot lines accurately to reaction highs and lows takes practice and a trained eye, but together with candlesticks it does becomes easier. They are an

Buying and Selling = Support and Resistance Levels 101

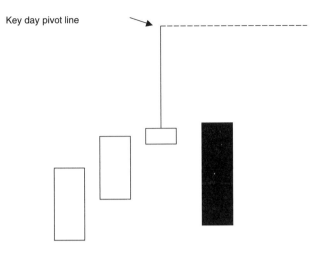

Exhibit 3.6 Feeling the market. A key day!

essential part of following market price action and should be used sparingly whenever the market looks to be topping or bottoming. It is during the trending phase of a market that the market is easier to follow and predict. However, once the market reaches a level of major resistance or support, it tends to become random and often unpredictable with volatile swings in both directions.

An important and very useful aspect of pivot lines is that they are most often found after a period of buying or selling is over, and although the price action moves away from the pivot line, the line itself eventually acts like a magnet drawing the price back towards that level. The level will then be tested again and again as the price rotates around the line until the market decides on a direction.

The price action in Figure 3.14 on page 103 is another example of how valuable a pivot line can become. This shows the level where the market rejects the price after a period of trending resulting in a negative day. This pivot line is later a key level for many trading sessions until at last there is a final day of contact with the level and the price action continuing to trend in the original direction.

Finding and using pivot lines takes practice but once these areas become familiar they are very useful. These levels create visual reference points on a chart and help decisively in forming a bias for market direction and as points of support and resistance to which the market is likely to return. Certain candlestick types such as shooting stars or hammers, which have a long shadow, demonstrate that the market has found a level that may become pivotal, but are an immediate clue to where market pressure exists currently. Range bound markets also have implications for the technical trader and finding a pivot line can play an important role when the break out occurs.

102 Trading and Investing in the Forex Market Using Chart Techniques

Key day pivot with a long shadow

The market falters at the pivot line

(source MetaQuotes Software Corp)

Figure 3.13   EUR/USD weekly chart and a key pivot line and stochastic divergence.

As with weekly and daily candlesticks, pivot lines that occur on a weekly chart also appear on the daily chart demonstrating resistance or support at the same level. The weekly chart can show the market reacting very nicely to a pivot line, as in Figure 3.19 on page 108, the weekly chart has same pivot line on the daily chart and is perhaps easier to follow by observing the daily candlestick at that level.

Some pivot lines no doubt see more than one touch before they are no longer valid, but other levels will continue to be useful for longer periods. This is really a case of placing the pivot line in the context of the bigger picture. Pivots are also

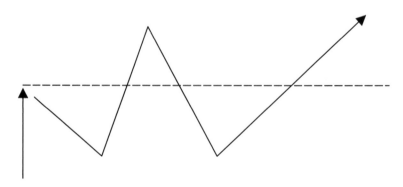

Exhibit 3.7   Key day pivot line.

Buying and Selling = Support and Resistance Levels   103

(source MetaQuotes Software Corp)

Figure 3.14 AUS/USD daily chart with pivot line acting like a magnet for price action. The pivot line continues to be significant for price action for many days until eventually the direction unfolds and the price moves away.

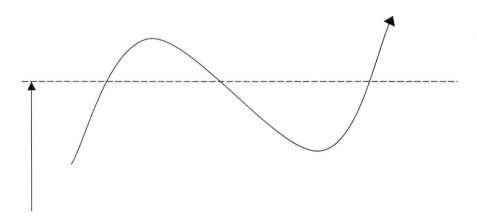

Exhibit 3.8 Pivot lines have a shorter duration than a trend line.

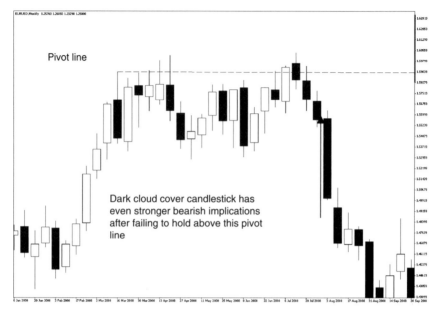

(source MetaQuotes Software Corp)

Figure 3.15 EUR/USD weekly chart with a pivot line that has directional implications as well as, in this example, strong resistance value.

a case of needing practice, becoming good at finding significant pivot lines make it easier to understand the context of the trend and the sentiment of the market at that time. They also assist decisively in placing certain candlestick types into the context of the actual market sentiment.

One important factor to remember about pivot lines is that they are most often found after a period of buying or selling is over, but although the price action moves away from the level the pivot line draws to price back to that level where it rotates and moves off. In Chapter 4, pivot lines are used in conjunction with the MACD-Histogram.

PREDETERMINED PIVOT HIGHS AND LOWS

Pivot levels are found not only at reaction highs or lows but also at predetermined days such as the first trading day of the month. To be able to apply these levels it is necessary to determine the opening and closing time of the daily session. However, because the forex market is for 24 hours there are often differing times between some charts. For the purposes of this book 12:00 pm GMT is used.

Buying and Selling = Support and Resistance Levels 105

(source MetaQuotes Software Corp)

Figure 3.16 EUR/USD daily chart with lots of candlestick patterns and signals but with no context.

By utilising the high and low of the first trading session of each month two very important lines on the chart are created which have directional implications for the entire month. Looking at the charts in Figures 3.16 (above) and 3.17 (overleaf) this becomes clear. The chart in Figure 3.16 is a typical candlestick chart. Figure 3.17 shows the same candlestick chart but the daily candlesticks are placed in the context of the high and low pivot lines applied to the first trading day of the month.

These predetermined lines create the directional bias going forward and by observing the daily candlestick at these levels one is watching for confirmation of the market price action finding resistance or support. Like the reaction high or low pivot, these predetermined pivot lines act as a barrier for price action which needs to break through and hold above or below the level in order to determine the direction.

For example, a rejection at the lower line suggests that the price action is likely to try for the upper line, a break out would then have greater significance because the price has already attempted the lower line. These areas also provide the technical trader with potential areas in which to place market stops loss orders.

There are many candlestick signals in Figure 3.17, which together with the first day of the month high and low pivot lines have more strength. The chart has another dimension.

(source MetaQuotes Software Corp)

Figure 3.17 The same EUR/USD daily chart as in Figure 3.16, showing candlestick patterns and signals, but placed in the context of the first trading day of the month.

If the market is trending down and a break out occurs to the upside, that is, the price breaks through the upper pivot line and then returns to the upper pivot line and eventually breaks below into the first day of the month range, the probability increases that the market will continue to the downside and continue to trend.

Now think about what would happen if a marabozu candle formed as the first day of the month. A marabozu candle often experiences retracement due to profit taking thus making the pivot high or low that much more effective as a directional bias and it also has a mid-point pivot line.

The chart in Figure 3.18 opposite shows how the first day of the month high and low pivot line determines market direction after the upper pivot line rejects the price action and captures the top of the trend quite well. In this example there is also a marabozu candlestick and therefore a mid-point pivot line that works quite well at holding back the market. Positions placed at this level could have a stop loss just above the upper pivot line. At the lower pivot line the market price action tends to cluster before eventually the final point of contact is made and the market moves lower. The lower pivot line is at that point the confirmation which a technical trader requires, that is, a final rejection to the upside allows another position to be added. The upper shadow of the final candle at the pivot line suggests that there were sellers positioned at the trend line. Likewise, the opening of the candle just below the pivot line is a good warning that the market is weakening.

Consider the large marabozu candle as being the first trading day of the month. A marabozu candle often experiences retracement due to profits being taken. Seeing

Buying and Selling = Support and Resistance Levels 107

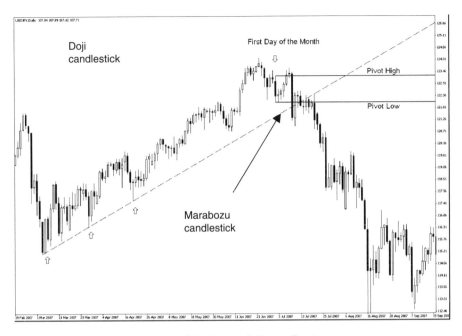

(source MetaQuotes Software Corp)

Figure 3.18 USD/JPY daily chart prices cluster around the lower pivot line until the market is finally rejected from that level.

such a candle type would add weight to the pivot line as being a point where the price will expect a rejection.

A chart on a short time frame displaying the pivot high and low of the first day of the month can make the task of interpreting price action easier. The daily chart in Figure 3.19 overleaf shows strong support and then strong resistance at the first day of the month high. This would act as a bias for market direction going forward. If the price gets above that level then it immediately becomes an area in which to observe the market for further directional confirmation. If, however, as in the example shown, the price returns to the lower level, the bias would be for lower price action. Although the price clusters at the lower level and this can become confusing, it should be seen as an advantage because at some point the price will break away from the cluster and as the upper line has already been rejected the bias would be for a break away to the down side! Filtering by waiting for two or three daily closes above or below the level will help to confirm the market conviction as will filtering by looking for a certain percentage to be reached above or below the line. These are discretional elements to trading and these have to be tested before applying these techniques.

The short-term chart example in Figure 3.18 demonstrates the pivot line that is based on the first hour of the trading week. The pivot line is taken from the high and

(source MetaQuotes Software Corp)

Figure 3.19 USD/JPY daily chart showing the first day of the month high and low.

low of the first hour which would be 12:00 pm GMT, and just like the high and low of the first trading day of the month, a direction bias is formed upon a complete break of one of the lines. Quite clearly, the reaction pivot line taken from the high of the hourly candlestick has proved that particular pivot line to be strong resistance, while the first hour pivot was the directional bias, in this case to the upside. The reaction pivot eventually has one final touch before the market sells off. The directional pivot, however, keeps the bias to the upside; as seen when the market approaches this level, buyers step in and push the market higher again.

It is a set up such as the example in Figure 3.20 opposite that has an effective impact on the overall market price enabling long-term investments to enter the market at optimal levels. Positioning strategic *stop orders* in the market is likewise easily achieved by watching the levels in order to reject the price. On the chart in Figure 3.20, the long-term trend is upwards, and the short-term chart suggests that the bear action to the downside might be over. A good area for positioning a market *stop order* would be below the pivot line of the first hour low. This example of the pivot line, applied as a form of money management, actually outweighs the importance placed on the levels as market entry opportunities. In this case, the technical trader would know where to exit the market if the strategy failed.

Buying and Selling = Support and Resistance Levels

(source MetaQuotes Software Corp)

Figure 3.20 EUR/JPY daily chart showing a classic pivot line and the first hour of the trading week high and low. Buyers step in and push the price higher as it approaches the first hour pivot again.

CALCULATED PIVOT LINES

These lines differ in that they are not seen but are instead created by calculation. A valuable method and one that is discussed in great detail in the work of Fisher (2002, p. 37), is the use of pivots taken by calculating the daily high, low and close and then calculating the high and low, and calculating the difference between the two numbers to form a core area that defines support or resistance for the current session based on the previous session. The current session has a directional bias once the core area is proven as support or resistance.

High	1.2681	
Close	1.2654	1.2645
Low	1.2602	= 4 point difference
High	1.2681	1.2641
Low	1.2602	

The pivot example is created by first subtracting the 4 point difference from the first sum and then adding the 4 point difference to the first sum. It would look like this:

1.2649

Pivot range

1.2641

Reprinted with permission of John Wiley & Sons, Inc.

Exhibit 3.9   How to calculate the core pivot line.

FIBONACCI LEVELS

Fibonacci levels are similar to finding old support and resistance levels but differ in design and application in that they provide important clues about future possible areas of support and resistance.

It was a twelfth century mathematician named Leonardo of Pisa who first introduced the numbering sequence but the discovery of certain ratios found throughout the natural world have long been known and incorporated within Egyptian and later Greek and Roman architecture. Today, however, the ratios are also found in the forex markets.

The Fibonacci levels are derived from the Fibonacci numbering system which is as follows: 1, 1, 2, 3, 5, 8, 13, 21, 34, 55, 89, 144. Quite simply, the sum of any two numbers equals the next highest number. By taking any number and dividing it by the next highest number, the sum comes out at around 0.618; divide any number by the preceding number and the sum equals 1.618. These two numbers are used in market analysis with great accuracy, and can lead to projected targets showing future areas

Buying and Selling = Support and Resistance Levels

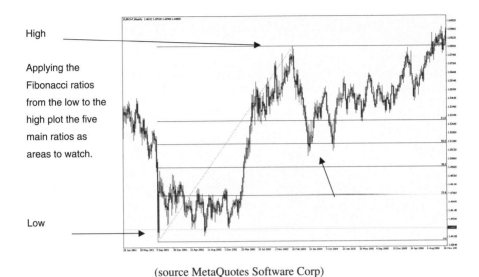

(source MetaQuotes Software Corp)

Figure 3.21 EUR/CHF weekly chart. Here the 50 % retracement level proves to be good support, being tested twice and forming a type of double bottom at the 50 % retracement level.

of support or resistance. The 61.8 % ratio is applied to a market in order to try and determine whether the market is correcting or reversing.

The (Golden) ratio 0.618 and 1.618, is as important today as it was in ancient times. To the Egyptians, Greeks and Romans, it was known as the Golden Section and was used within the construction of the Pyramids and the Parthenon to give a greater aesthetic value to the architecture. Today it is still as significant and can be seen everywhere, from shapes and forms found in nature to applications in music, art and architecture. The sequence has a great aesthetic value but the value of the ratios, especially the Golden Section, is more than just aesthetic in the financial markets, it is where support and resistance levels are found. The ratios 23.6 %, 38.2 %, 50 %, 61.8 % and 76.4 %, are commonly applied to charts in order to determine levels of support and resistance during a correction with 61.8 % (the Golden ratio) as the most important ratio. In this chapter the following methods are discussed: Fibonacci retracement levels, Fibonacci projection levels.

The first and most useful application of the Fibonacci system is to find an important high, retrace that move to the original low and apply the sequence from high to low and find levels of support during market corrections. The opposite applies in a downwards trend. The example in Figure 3.21, shows how the retracement ratios are used to signal areas where support may be found during a correction after the market has experienced a substantial move upwards.

In Figure 3.22 overleaf, the 61.8 % level (the Golden Ratio), held the price during a short-term retracement. However, if the price fails to hold at the 61.8 %

(source MetaQuotes Software Corp)

Figure 3.22 GBP/JPY weekly chart. The 61.8% retracement zone holding as support signalled by a hammer candlestick.

level, a full retracement can be expected. The 61.8% level is also very helpful for determining the strength of a trend. For example, a correction might provide the technical trader with an opportunity to begin placing positions in the market. The Fibonacci levels can help to determine the most likely areas of support and resistance.

The chart in Figure 3.22 shows how the Fibonacci retracement ratios support the market price at the 61.8% level leading to a more bullish stance in the market. Applying a trend line tentatively to the second reaction low and monitoring the Fibonacci ratios after that low would help enormously in maintaining the view that the market will continue to move higher. The idea that there could be a trend line forming that would lead to participating in a trending market which later develops from that price level, is supported by the fact that the 61.8% level supports the price action as do the 50% and 38.2% levels later on.

The Golden Ratio in chart analysis is very important for finding a level on the chart where the market price action may falter. If it does not then this may be a sign of weakness in the current trend as the correction goes deeper than anticipated. There is normally a reaction at these levels, at least on the first test of each level, but it is 61.8% that is the most significant level and the level that determines the market's strength or weakness. If price action during a correction fails to hold at this level of

Buying and Selling = Support and Resistance Levels 113

(source MetaQuotes Software Corp)

Figure 3.23 USD/CAD daily chart with Fibonacci retracement levels.

61.8%, then a full retracement can be expected. The first significant close below the 61.8 % level is the first clue (the opposite in a bearish market).

Remember, it is always important to confirm an area of support or resistance by finding other technical aspects that fit and confirm that price level. For example, if the 61.8 % Fibonacci level is very close to a previous pivot line or trend line, then that line is probably much stronger as a level of support or resistance on the chart.

As long as there is a defined high and low, the Fibonacci retracement levels (see Figure 3.23) can be applied. The ratios can likewise be used in a range bound market creating a framework of support and resistance levels that might be significant during the entire period that the market remains range bound.

The Fibonacci levels are applied to range bound markets helping to determine exactly where the potential support and resistance level might be found. Figure 3.23 shows the spot gold market trading above and below the 50 % level before finally moving much higher. The 50 % level is polarity and sees the price react at the higher and lower Fibonacci ratios but always returning to the 50 % level before moving much higher.

Another slightly more complicated use of Fibonacci numbers on charts is to find a high and low and then project forward by adding the Golden Ratio of 61.8 % once the market breaks out above the old high to create a possible price objective. This method of analysing the market for future projected areas of support or resistance requires experience and it is advisable to go over Figure 3.24 overleaf and try to find areas where the projection worked well. In Figure 3.25 overleaf, the projection was

(source MetaQuotes Software Corp)

Figure 3.24 Spot gold daily chart demonstrating the use of Fibonacci levels as support and resistance point on a long-term basis.

very useful for producing a projected target. The price finds resistance and support and eventually clusters around the 200 % projected Fibonacci ratio.

Applying the ratios and extending the ratio results in Fibonacci levels appearing at future points in time where the market may find a reaction. The projection is estab-

(source MetaQuotes Software Corp)

Figure 3.25 EUR/USD daily chart demonstrating a Fibonacci projection.

Buying and Selling = Support and Resistance Levels

(source MetaQuotes Software Corp)

Figure 3.26 EUR/JPY daily chart with a primary Fibonacci projection and a minor projection level appearing at the same level which confirms that price zone as being an important level to watch.

lished by first finding an established high and an established low, as in Figure 3.25, then adding the ratios 23.6%, 38.2%, 50%, 61.8% and 76.4%, but only once the market breaks above the previous high. By doing this you would achieve 123.6%, 138.2%, 150%, 161.8%, and 176.4%.

As with all confirmation techniques it is very useful for the technical trader to find more than one technical aspect as confirmation. This also applies to lines that converge at the same price level and to Fibonacci ratios which are seen converging at the same level. In Figure 3.26, the Fibonacci ratios are projected upwards, twice. This is achieved by taking the high and low of a short-term trend and measuring this range of activity which can then be used as a projection forwards creating a target. The price has to push past the previous high or low first and confirm the break higher or lower before applying the projection. By adding 61.8% to the ratio, a projected target is reached equal to 1.618. Later, by adding another projection, typically measured from a correction, ratios can often appear at or close to the same price level. In the example in Figure 3.26, the ratios 38.2% and 61.8% appear at the same level. When ratios appear together like this they may have a far stronger impact on the price action.

Applying the Fibonacci retracement levels to the high and the low (resistance and support) is suitable for the projection. However, it may be more accurate occasionally by looking for a key pivot line instead of the absolute high or low. One method of determining the accuracy of levels is by studying the levels and seeing how well they fit within the Fibonacci retracement frame.

(source MetaQuotes Software Corp)

Figure 3.27 USD/JPY daily chart showing a Fibonacci level taken from the low to a pivot high. If the price fits within the frame it can be applied.

The best way to try this is to go over charts and try fitting the Fibonacci ratios, as in the example in Figure 3.27. The levels are from the low to the first key pivot line as the high of the move but not the actual high of the intermediate trend!

The reason that pivot lines provide suitable areas to measure the market for a correction and therefore the potential support levels is that usually up to the point where the pivot line is found the market has seen a very dynamic move. One of the best methods of using a pivot is to watch the market rotate at this level; this simply would suggest by definition that the market is no longer as dynamic as it was during the trending phase.

The candlestick signals that appear at Fiboannci ratios will have more emphasis as they are seen in the context of the measured moves. Generally these levels can be precise enough to think about entering a position at or close to the opening of the day's session, believing that the Fibonacci level will continue to hold. A very good method of finding the precise area of support or resistance at an early stage is to lay the measurement first from the high to the low and then add a second framework from the close of that high to the open of the low.

In Figure 3.29 on page 118, the chart shows a good example of how the measurement is precise when applying the ratios not only to the highs and lows but to the open and close. The 61.8 % level measured from the close down to the open finds the market reacting to that level as resistance more precisely than the 61.8 % level measured from the high to the low. This is a very useful clue, in this case, that the market will make a full retracement. The close to the open 50 % retracement level also made a very good area of support during the first part of the correction. Technically,

Buying and Selling = Support and Resistance Levels

(source MetaQuotes Software Corp)

Figure 3.28 EUR/JPY weekly chart with Fibonacci levels and candlestick signals.

it is viable to filter the moves across Fibonacci levels by a certain percentage or a certain number of consecutive closes. But as with many aspects of technical trading, this relies primarily on the discretion of the technical trader. The levels in the example in Figure 3.29 also create stop levels that are quite good. If the 50 % measurement based on the close to the open is holding during a correction, the 50 % measurement from the high to the low may be suitable for placing stop orders!

In spite of the huge sell off in the market, Figure 3.30 on page 118 shows how the 61.8 % level held the market which eventually produced a close above the 50 % level. Although the price opened above the 50 % level, the market tested the level before resuming the trend. It will be impossible to know fully whether or not a trend will resume during such a correction, and a huge sell like that can not only shake out positions from the market but also create uncertainty on a grand scale.

(source MetaQuotes Software Corp)

Figure 3.29 USD/JPY daily chart with Fibonacci levels taken from the high to the low and from the close of the high to the open of the low.

(source MetaQuotes Software Corp)

Figure 3.30 AUS/USD weekly chart with Fibonacci retracement ratios at work.

Buying and Selling = Support and Resistance Levels 119

(source MetaQuotes Software Corp)

Figure 3.31 USD/JPY daily chart with trend line and Fibonacci retracement ratios. The price tends to cluster the 61.8 % level.

The example in Figure 3.31 shows a good upward trend line that has been validated on three occasions by price testing the support line during the early part of the trend. Eventually there is a clear break leading to a complete and decisive change of market direction. There are, however, a number of clues such as the bearish marabozu candlestick, this closed below the first day of the month pivot low. The market eventually closes below the trend line and finds resistance at the first day of the month pivot low before accelerating lower. Clearly, this market was not prepared to stop at the 61.8 % Fibonacci retracement level. The fact that the market had been at the level for quite some time signifies the importance of the 61.8 % ratio but the market eventually declines beyond that level to produce a full retracement.

CHART ANALYSIS EXERCISE 3

In Figure 3.32 find the following:

- Bullish trend line;
- Intermediate trend line;
- Bullish triangle;
- Bullish flag.

Candlestick signals:

- Bearish engulfing;
- Piercing pattern;
- Tweezer;
- Hanging man;
- Dark cloud cover;
- Spinning top;
- Hammer.

(source MetaQuotes Software Corp)

Figure 3.32 EUR/USD daily chart in a upward trending market.

CHART ANALYSIS EXERCISE 3 – ANSWERS

(source MetaQuotes Software Corp)

Figure 3.33 EUR/USD daily chart with technical aspects.

These are just some of the straightforward techniques discussed so far. The most suitable way to learn the techniques so that they become familiar is to take a chart and go through it looking for signals, learn to see how the signals can vary in size and shape and determine how the signals occasionally require more time before producing the desired effect.

CHART ANALYSIS EXERCISE 4

In Figure 3.34 find the following:

- Key pivot line;
- Internal trend line;
- False break out;
- Double bottom;
- Marabozu candlestick;
- Hanging man;
- Spinning top;
- Harami;
- Bearish engulfing;
- Bullish engulfing;
- Piercing pattern.

(source MetaQuotes Software Corp)

Figure 3.34 AUS/USD daily chart exercise.

CHART ANALYSIS EXERCISE 4 – ANSWERS

(source MetaQuotes Software Corp)

Figure 3.35 AUS/USD daily chart.

SUMMARY

In this chapter the concept of support and resistance (polarity) has been discussed while demonstrating that areas of resistance later become areas of support in an upward tending market and areas of support later become areas of resistance in a downward trending market.

A trend line must have at least two points of contact, three is better. A trend channel requires three points of contact with one reaction low or high at the opposite side to begin the channel before the width can be determined. The more a trend line is tested the more valid it becomes until broken. This also applies to intermediate trend lines and internal trend lines, both of which are useful for finding consolidation, false break outs and break outs that lead to a continuation in trend. The intermediate trend lines in conjunction with candlestick are very good for finding failed break outs that produce a warning about current market sentiment. Internal trend lines are best positioned when the market is difficult to follow, consolidating or forming a potential pattern; basically they are a level to observe for eventual market conviction in a direction.

Observations show that pivot lines determine where the price action turns positive or negative creating a bullish or bearish bias; a failed break out back through a pivot line in a up trend (or down trend) is a sign that there is uncertainty in the trend at that present time and can be a forerunner to an intermediate trend line. Pivot lines have a magnetic effect on price action. After the price action has moved away from the level the market often returns to that level until there is a final touch at which point the direction is determined and the market moves off. Pivotal days are found at the high and low of the first trading day of each month. The high and low create a level to watch for market direction. This is best observed by placing a line at the high and low of the first day of each month and observing how the market reacts at these levels.

Fibonacci ratios are based on a mathematical sequence with 0.618 and 1.618 being the most significant levels; they are also known as the golden numbers. Identifying support and resistance areas using the standard retracements, which are 23.6 %, 38.2 %, 50 %, 61.8 % and 76.4 % is standard in the financial industry.

Fibonacci ratios make it possible to judge which market levels will become important during market corrections. These ratios appear at levels where the market will find potential support or resistance and may be incorporated with an investment strategy that allows the technical trader to take advantage of market corrections in areas where the market is essentially offering very good risk/reward opportunities.

Applying a filter can sometimes be very efficient when using Fibonacci levels, but only up to a certain point after which discretion must be applied; as with patterns there is a point where the trade must be discretionary. Filters, such as two or three consecutive closes, or even a weekly close above or below a level, are helpful in determining the strength of the ratio itself.

The Fibonacci ratios are unique for projecting forward and finding areas that will have some future significance for the price action. Likewise, these projections placed correctly demonstrate quite clearly future levels of support or resistance. Applying this technique also creates price objectives against which the market can be measured for signs of weakness, filtering the move past a Fibonacci ratio by a certain percentage or by the amount of pips. Likewise, the candlestick type and the closing level are useful methods for determining the conviction of the market at such levels.

As with all chart techniques using just one technique is not as reliable as multiple techniques. Applying further techniques to the chart is a process that builds greater confidence in the decision-making process. If there are two or three technical levels at a similar price zone, then these are important levels going forward. The candlestick pattern at such levels, where there are also multiple indications of an important level, can produce a stronger signal. It is equally important to find areas where the price fails to touch an area of resistance or support.

The previous chapters have shown that patterns and candlesticks produce opportunities in the financial markets and that by training the eye to find these signals together with areas of support and resistance it is possible to identify areas of great opportunity in the market at an early stage. Corrections offer suitable areas to join a trend and a trend is where the majority of the profit is made. It is unwise to trade against the primary trend.

4
Applying Confirmation = Confidence Building

Applying additional techniques to the chart is adding confidence to your decision-making process. A candlestick pattern or a chart pattern may signal a turning point in the market but as with most tasks that involve risk some form of confirmation will support the initial decision-making process further.

In this chapter the following technical indicators are covered:

- Single moving average;
- Double moving average;
- Moving average high and low;
- Momentum indicators, RSI, Stochastic and MACD.

Analysing daily charts for long-term price objectives by finding trend lines and observing the daily highs and lows against the line or finding a bullish continuation pattern helps to define the overall market sentiment. Observing the market at price levels where major support or resistance is likely to surface prepares the way for taking advantage of opportunities as and when they arise. It is about creating a technical plan with some option left open about market direction but it is also about being prepared for a change in the market so as to provide an edge. Finding the most likely area ahead of the price action where change is likely to happen can be difficult, but there are techniques that make this part of chart analysis easier to follow.

SIMPLE MOVING AVERAGE (SMA)

The moving average is the interpretation of the market price action over a set period of time on any time frame and is used to smooth out the price action for that chosen

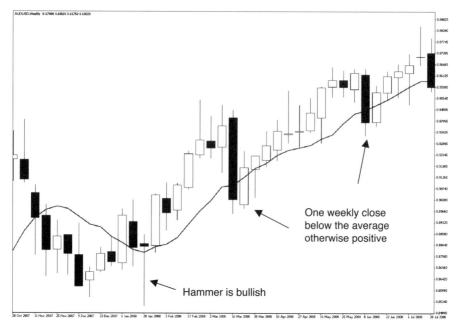

(source MetaQuotes Software Corp)

Figure 4.1 AUS/USD weekly chart illustrating just how useful this single moving average can be for following a market. The hammer provides bullish incentive with only two closes registered below the 10-week average until the doji signal.

period in time. The simple moving average is the interpretation of price action at current levels based on arbitrary parameters. The simple moving average forms a visual level that supports the current price, confirms the current trend, or establishes a change in the current state of that market.

Figure 4.1 shows a market that is trending higher, higher highs and higher lows. Apart from dips below the average price the closing price is more often than not above the moving average. Together with Japanese candlesticks this displays a market that is finding buying pressure each time the market moves towards the average price, in this case, the 10-week average. A market that is trending higher tends to remain above the moving average and below it when the market is trending downwards. This method of observing price action in relation to the price action of a set period is especially good for monitoring the market. The low and especially the close in relation to the moving average allow the position to be monitored for any signs of weakness. A potential change in market direction can be tested by filtering the price against the moving average by watching for a close or a series of consecutive closes below or above the average line as a signal.

A first initial close may be the initial clue but would need to have some other form of confirmation. Visually, however, the moving average allows many markets to be observed quickly for signs of weakness or change that can picked out and validated through other chart techniques in order to confirm the initial signal of the moving average. The averages are unique in that they can define as well as confirm existing areas of support or resistance but also show where market divergence is appearing.

The moving average is probably the simplest of systems in both its generation and form and is visually very clear on the chart. A simple moving average is produced by taking a price, usually the closing price, although the high or the low or the average of all three can also be adequate methods for producing moving averages. From a set number of days, for example 10 days, the base price to be averaged, usually the closing price for the period, is totalled and divided by the same period in order to reach the average price for a set period of days or weeks. The following session and the furthest price is dropped and the latest price is added to the equation; in this manner the average price is found and continues to produce the average price for a set period, as in the example given in Figure 4.1.

The calculation may look like this: if the period being used is a period of 10 days, the closing price of the previous 10 days is totalled and then divided by 10 to reach the average price for a period of 10 days. The following session and the furthest price is dropped and the latest price added to the equation.

Some examples of moving average periods used in the industry are 5, 10, 20, 30 and 90. These values are applied to correspond to the number of days or weeks being applied to the chart analysis. The two week, the working month, the entire month and the quarter period and important time periods of the working year such a monthly or quarterly can easily be represented in this manner. Other numbers applied to moving averages are the Fibonacci numbers, 5, 8, 13, 21, 34, 55, etc. It becomes a case of finding numbers that work in the markets in which you trade.

Every technician has a preference and applies their own set period; usually a number has been back tested against either the closing price or the high or low in order to find the most reliable number. The numbers are arbitrary, however, whatever set numbers are applied, and they must be used consistently within chart analysis. Simply changing the period of the average because the average fits the price will produce false signals.

The moving average criterion is best set according to each market. For example, the eight-day and 28-day moving average are quite good on the price of EUR/USD, but 10-day and 30-day work adequately on all forex markets, as well as the weekly time frame. The moving average is usually based on the closing price but in a 24-hour market such as the forex market it is likely to be more suitable to use the average daily price and incorporate this into a moving average system. For example, calculating the daily high/low/close and dividing by three will yield the average daily price. This method incorporates the core of the day's trading and is used in the moving average equation instead of the closing price. This may not be necessary for weekly averages as there is a definitive close and open for the weekly price.

Another very useful method of averaging the price is to apply two moving averages and watch for a cross over, either positive or negative.

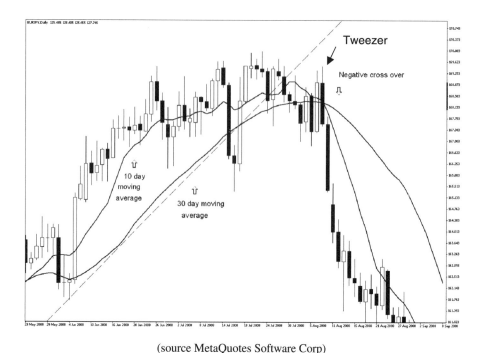

(source MetaQuotes Software Corp)

Figure 4.2 EUR/JPY daily chart showing the negative cross over of the 10-day moving average and the 30-day moving average. This demonstrates clearly how moving averages can confirm a change in market direction.

Applying two averages is a technique used by many professionals in the industry. The shorter time frame such as the 10-day period used on the chart in Figure 4.2 helps to confirm the trend while it is above the long-term 30-day moving average. The crossing of the averages is seen as a signal that the market is changing direction but caution should be applied to this method. Just because the averages have crossed does not prove that the market price action will change direction; a cross over does, however, warn of a possible change in market direction. Observing the averages as they come together would prepare the technical trader for a change in market direction. The 10 and 30-day moving average can be used to monitor the strength of the trend. A cross over of the two averages warns about the current state of that trend.

The moving average, however, is a lagging indicator. It is therefore necessary to understand that it does not lead the market. The price action is smoothed out, which as a tool for the chart can underscore the price action if a market is trending. However, its main use is in helping to determine the health of a trend.

There are other types of moving average such as the linear weighted moving average and the exponentially weighted moving average. These are not discussed in this book simply because the premise of this training manual is based on the simple

Applying Confirmation = Confidence Building

observation of daily price action as it is each day rather than giving greater emphasis to the more recent price action.

The advantage of the simple moving average as a confirmation tool is the fact that it is based on the number of days. By using this method and being consistent with a set number of days, say for example, five for five working days of the week, or 30 days for an average month, it is possible to create an overall picture of price action over a set period and observe it against the average price for signs of change to the support or resistance levels that the averages create. The averages will point out areas of support and resistance and provide important clues as to market sentiment when these areas are penetrated. A second or third daily close above or below an average can be an important clue about the market and a potential change in market sentiment. The moving average is a very visual and very objective method of understanding current price action. The moving average is most useful when the market is trending and will tend to give false signals in a sideways market.

The main uses of the moving average are:

1. Direction – the continued price action above or below the average confirms a trending market. Once a market starts to trend the price action may move further away from the average and then correct back towards the average price, which can be misleading. But as long as the price remains above the average the trend should continue.
2. At the end of a trending market the averages become very significant. The first close below an average in an up trend can be a useful clue to a change in market sentiment.

As Figure 4.3 overleaf demonstrates, the price action on the 10-day average finds resistance at the average itself and later tends to cluster at the level where the market is changing from a downwards direction to a range based market. The resistance area is now above the average instead of at the average price and there are gradually closes at and above the average price level. There are some bullish engulfing days that push the price above the average but the market is changing from bearish to range bound. However, observing the daily price against the average allows the market to be monitored for signs of change on a daily basis!

The 10-day moving average and the 30-day moving average, as shown in Figure 4.4 overleaf, cross negative displaying a decisive change in market sentiment. But watching for consecutive daily closes above both averages, especially the 30-day average, would have revealed whether or not the negative cross might fail to see price action follow through. When the price is seen clinging to the averages after the averages have crossed, and registering daily closes above the short-term average, in this example the 10-day moving average, that is usually a sign that the market is not decisive enough to follow the direction of the cross over. There were, however, no closes registered above the 10-day or 30-day average after they crossed over. In this example a clear change of market direction followed.

(source MetaQuotes Software Corp)

Figure 4.3 EUR/USD daily chart with 10-day, 30-day and 90-day moving averages based on the daily closing price.

(source MetaQuotes Software Corp)

Figure 4.4 USD/JPY daily chart with two averages, the 10-day and 30-day moving average. The market sentiment has changed notably when the 10-day average crosses below the 30-day average.

Applying Confirmation = Confidence Building

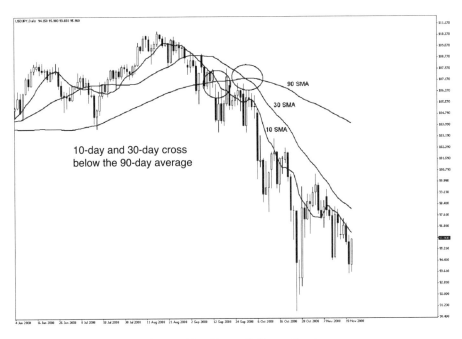

(source MetaQuotes Software Corp)

Figure 4.5 USD/JPY daily chart with 10, 30 and 90-day simple moving averages crossing negative.

After a turn in the market, the price action might still attempt to move above (or below) an average but the final rejection of the market should be found in order to confirm the resistance (or support) of that moving average. Apply a filter of three consecutive daily closes above (or below) the average. This should be achieved before attempting to enter the market based on the moving average cross over. Admittedly, some cross overs are quite quick and the price action simply moves away very fast, but this type of market may already be over bought or over sold and showing signs of divergence. However, once the market has established a new direction, a good moving average will show the price finding support (during an upward trend) or resistance (in a downward tend).

The 90-day simple moving average is a long-term indicator. This may, however, be incorporated adequately within daily technical analysis by using the 90-day average as a type of barometer for confirming the long-term market direction and for clearing any uncertainty in the market. As long as the price is above the 90-day average the main trend remains upwards and when the price is below the average the trend is downwards. However, the 90-day average is also similar to the pivot line in that the price tends to take long swings around the 90-day average line. The price will move away for a period and then return.

(source MetaQuotes Software Corp)

Figure 4.6 The 90-day simple moving average shows prices returning to the average and then moving away from the average only to return again until eventually price clusters around the average.

In the example shown in Figure 4.6, the price bounces off the 90-day simple moving average but the average attracts the price action back again until the price action remains at the average, clustering around that level until pushing through it decisively and beyond. The long-term trend is down until such time as the price action is seen to hold above the average. Additionally, the small channel found in the downward trend acts as a point where the price falters to the downside, finds support and then gains momentum back towards the 90-day average. Although some market technicians may not agree on the trend channel shown in Figure 4.6, the three points necessary to form the channel are found at the start of the downward phase and on closer inspection of the price action against the channel, the lines are validated. More often than not!

SIMPLE MOVING AVERAGE CHANNEL

Another useful application of the moving average based indicator is to set the parameters of the calculation to the highs and lows of the price action. Setting the

Applying Confirmation = Confidence Building   133

(source MetaQuotes Software Corp)

Figure 4.7 USD/JPY with the 10-day moving average based on the low and the high of the last 10 sessions. This way the averages produce a confirmation signal after the break of the trend line, which for many traders and investors would be a sell signal. However, the price tends to congest shortly after the break below the trend line which can be confusing and lead to profit taking too early into the move. The upper band, however, suggests resistance and there is no reason to get out of a short position.

parameters to calculate the high or the low creates a channel of average price. This produces channels of support and resistance and confirms market direction by containing the price action above and within the channel or below and within the channel. A move above or below followed by two or three consecutive closes above or below the channel can warn of a change in direction.

The moving average based on the high and low shows exactly where the areas of support and resistance are. Visually they are very effective as Figure 4.8 overleaf demonstrates. The 30-day low becomes resistance during the negative cross over, and later becomes support during the positive cross over. It is this type of technical scenario that will help the technical trader to identify areas where the market is presenting an opportunity. The chart in Figure 4.9 overleaf also demonstrates how an area of support later becomes an area of resistance.

The example in Figure 4.9 shows how the 10-day moving average channel tends to see price action below the moving average low during the downwards trend and during the downwards trend the 10-day high/low average moves away from the 30-day high/low average. The bias would be to initiate short positions on up ticks towards the 10-day average high while the gap between the averages is widening. Once the averages come together the bias would be to remain neutral. Range

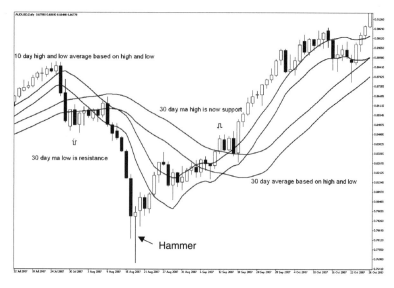

(source MetaQuotes Software Corp)

Figure 4.8 The 10 and 30-day moving averages based on the high and low of the period. The short-term channel average crosses the long-term average generating a positive or negative market bias.

(source MetaQuotes Software Corp)

Figure 4.9 EUR/USD daily chart. The 10-day high/low moving average comes together with the 30-day moving average. The 90-day would become a viable target.

Applying Confirmation = Confidence Building

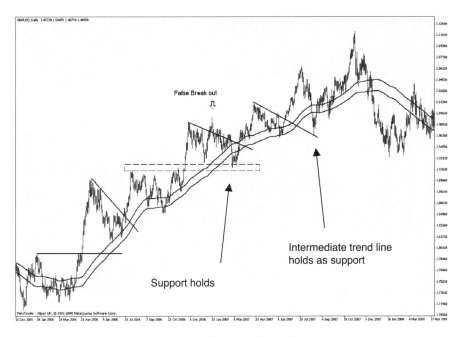

(source MetaQuotes Software Corp)

Figure 4.10 GBP/USD daily chart. The 90-day high/low average becomes a useful directional indicator. Above the average and the bias is bullish; below the 90-day average and the bias is bearish. Intermediate trend lines and break outs maintain the directional bias.

bound markets would only see short-term trades, buying against the low and selling against the high scenario. When the market becomes range bound the short-term moving average channel contains all the price action for a while. But once the 30-day average channel joins the 10-day moving average channel the price is contained within the high of the long-term 30-day average and the low of the 10-day average low.

The markets are not always so obliging. In Figure 4.10, the 90-day high/low determines the direction quite well, maintaining the bias to remain long. The market price dips into the channel only to find support. Although in this example the price has seen activity below the lower channel, there are more dips into the channel where support has been found than there are price dips below the channel. To confirm a break below the channel the price would have to move away sufficiently from the lower line and break below other support levels or see consecutive closes below the line. The bias remains to the upside even though the price action below the lower low would cause some longs to exit their positions.

Figure 4.11 overleaf shows how the market, once back above the average, finds support at the base of the 90-day moving average channel. The market has seen a

136   Trading and Investing in the Forex Market Using Chart Techniques

(source MetaQuotes Software Corp)

Figure 4.11 USD/JPY daily chart with 90-day high/low moving average channel as support and directional indicator.

double bottom form which pushed prices higher into the channel, after which the price clusters around the upper channel line. There was a final touch with the lower channel line before prices eventually moved higher. Later, the 90-day channel provides support and helps confirms the market direction; together with the intermediate trend lines and support and resistance, it serves as a good overall indicator. It is sensible to observe the market as it approaches the high or low when using the average as a channel.

The trending environment is where the majority of professional investors and traders will be found as this is the environment where the greatest profit is made. Looking at USD/JPY in Figure 4.12 opposite, it becomes apparent that the 90-day high/low simple moving average provides not only support but also a directional bias. What is interesting, however, is that the first day of the month high/low pivot experienced a downward break out into the moving average channel only to find support before turning around and breaking out to the upside. Together with a straightforward support line and an intermediate trend line that has experienced a false break out leaving a tweezer pattern, the market has direction. This type of scenario repeats itself in the markets, especially in a trending environment, and is of great value to the technical trader.

Applying Confirmation = Confidence Building

(source MetaQuotes Software Corp)

Figure 4.12 USD/JPY daily chart in a trending market. Support comes in at the 90-day high/low average. The first day of the month pivot high/low provides a good directional clue.

CHART ANALYSIS EXERCISE 5

Find the following in Figure 4.13 overleaf

1. Hammer = feeling the market and rejecting the downside.
2. Bullish engulfing = pushes the price above the averages.
   (1 & 2 are also first two contact points of a trend line)
3. Ten-day and 30-day averages cross positive.
4. Slight slippage below the 10-day average but close above on next trading session.
5. Ten day average holds as support = Trend intact.
6. Useful pivot point provides confidence once cleared.
7. Another pivot point with more immediate significance.
8. Price action struggles at the pivot point level.
9. Three days below 10-day moving average = warning of a possible top, bring up stop loss order to first pivot line at no. 6
10. Price action gets back over 10-day moving average which holds and the price moves back above pivot point plus.

11. Price action feeling the market. Also a good point at which to place a pivot line.
12. Tweezer top followed by hanging man = warning of possible top.
13. Pivot point holds and price action has seven days below the 10-day moving average – the longest amount of time since the beginning of the trend.
14. Two days back above the 10-average and still below the pivot point and a harami = reversal in direction.
15. Ten day moving average crossing below the 30-day moving average is negative.
16. Price action is below a previous pivot point.
17. Hammer and bullish engulfing day push price action higher.
18. Harami against 50 % Fibonacci retracement = resistance.
19. Price action congestion at previous pivot point level and 30-day average = resistance.
20. Double bottom pushes price action back above 10-day average.
21. Averages cross positive on bullish engulfing day.
22. Previous pivot becomes immediate support .

(source MetaQuotes Software Corp)

Figure 4.13 GBP/USD daily chart with 10 and 30-day moving average showing the negative and positive cross over.

Applying Confirmation = Confidence Building 139

(source MetaQuotes Software Corp)

Figure 4.14 GBP/USD daily chart with technical answers.

CHART ANALYSIS EXERCISE 5 – ANSWERS

The answers to the above are illustrated in Figure 4.14. The moving average presents a very visual picture of support and resistance in comparison to other techniques, and also displays the overall market sentiment. Used properly and consistently this technique will be of great value as a confirmation tool and the more techniques there are pointing at the same level and confirming that level as being important the easier the decision-making process will be in the long run.

Changing the indicators' parameters to fit the picture will result in false signals and for this reason it is sensible to try out different averages and observe how the market reacts at or around those numbers. The more the average is touched the greater the validity the moving average will have as an indicator.

MOMENTUM OSCILLATORS

The momentum oscillator is a computer generated technical tool designed primarily for use within a range bound market. As with any indicator, whether computer generated or self made, the signal should be easy to read, making the decision to buy or sell on a market that much easier. The most useful readings are seen when the oscillator generates an over-sold or over-bought signal, i.e. extremes. It is used also by setting the parameters typically between 0–100 and watching for the oscillator to cross the lines at these parameters.

Price action is the basis of chart reading and it is from daily price action that the momentum oscillator's signals are generated. The momentum oscillator is intended for use in sideways markets and it is a lagging indicator, that is, the indicator is secondary to price action! Momentum oscillators have parameters with set variables which are used to create the parameters. These parameters then measure the speed of change within the price action itself.

For example, if the daily price action is moving higher per daily session and the momentum oscillator is rising, then the higher price action is confirmed by the momentum. If the momentum begins to flatten out or is an over-bought condition this can be a sign of a pause in price action. When the momentum oscillator begins to decline and price action is still moving higher this is a sign that the higher price action is losing its momentum.

These indicators are based on moving averages which are lagging indicators by the nature of their construction. However, the momentum indicator, when moving in the opposite direction to current price action, actually becomes a leading indicator. This is one of the greatest advantages of the momentum oscillator when used for finding divergence.

There are three main ways to use momentum oscillators:

- Direction – this usually confirms a trending market. Once a market starts to trend, however, this indicator may already be over bought or over sold and can therefore be misleading. But the opposite is true at the end of a trending market where these indicators become very significant.
- Over bought/over sold – this suggests that the market is at extreme levels. For example, the price action in a market that has been trending higher for some time has more buying demand than selling pressure. Eventually there will be no more buyers available to join the current trend. The same applies to the downside.
- Divergence – this by its very definition becomes a leading indicator. Divergence shows that the market is reaching or has reached the conditions mentioned above, but that the price action is beginning to slow. It is usually a good warning that a market top or bottom could soon be reached as the price action continues to rise and the indicator does not. The same occurs with a market that makes new lows and where the momentum indicator does not follow.

THE RSI OSCILLATOR

The RSI oscillator was created by J. Wells Wilder, Jr. This indicator is designed to compare the average gains on those days where the market has closed positive with the average loss where the market has closed negative. Figure 4.15 opposite shows

Applying Confirmation = Confidence Building

(source MetaQuotes Software Corp)

Figure 4.15 EUR/USD daily chart shows how the over-bought and over-sold conditions are displayed, but its greatest value is when the indicator produces divergence. This becomes a leading indicator.

how the RSI oscillator produces over-sold conditions (at 1, 2 and 3), that are actually buy signals and then eventually produces divergence. The prices continue to move higher (4) and (5) but the RSI does not, at this point the RSI has become a leading indicator. The final high is, likewise, a bearish engulfing candlestick.

Again the opposite applies when the price action moves lower, as with the AUS/USD. At point (1) prices have moved lower but the RSI at point (2) has failed to make a new low. At this point there is divergence. This is where the RSI oscillator is working at its best, when divergence occurs at over-bought/over-sold levels.

Note: The RSI, during a strong trend, will tend to be in the over-bought/over-sold level for longer periods of time and therefore likely to produce signals that can lead to closing a position too soon! If a market is trending strongly for a long period of time the RSI can remain at extreme levels, especially in the over-bought reading.

THE STOCHASTIC OSCILLATOR (SLOW)

The Stochastic momentum indicator was designed by George Lane during the 1950s. Observation of rising price action shows that the closing price tends to be near the

(source MetaQuotes Software Corp)

Figure 4.16 AUS/USD daily chart shows how divergence forms in this example as the market price action makes a new low but the indicator does not.

highs of the day, the opposite applies in a market with lower price action. As with the RSI, there are over-bought and over-sold levels with parameters that are set usually at 80/20 (75/25) indicated by two lines. Turning at the levels signals over done market conditions, but the Stochastic, unlike the RSI indicator, has two lines: %K and %D.

The %K represents the fast line and the %D the slow line, also known as the trigger line. The %K line is set to a certain number of days, for example a 10-day period would calculate the most recent close, against the highest high and the lowest low for that 10-day period, and demonstrate where the current close is in relation to the high/low of that period. The faster line %D represents the moving average for that period of %K and is likewise set to a certain period, for example six days against 10 and would trigger buy or sell when the %D crosses the %K line. Back testing to find the most suitable time period is recommended, however for the examples shown in this book 9, 6, 6 or 10, 6, 6, have been used. The industry standard seems to be 14 days, but working around a period of 10 days works just as well and is slightly more sensitive.

The stochastic indicator parameters are usually set at 80/20 (70/30). This is similar to the RSI but differs slightly in that there is also the crossing of the lines at the over-bought and over-sold level with a strong signal being produced if both lines are crossing and pointing in the same direction.

Applying Confirmation = Confidence Building

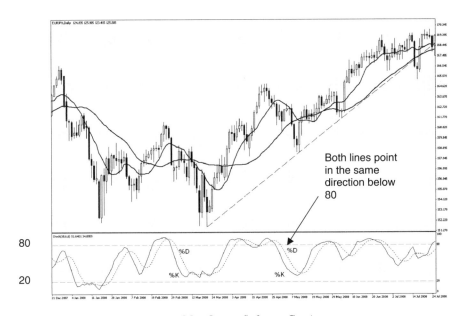

(source MetaQuotes Software Corp)

Figure 4.17 EUR/JPY daily chart showing the crossing of the lines at over-sold and over-bought levels. The signal is stronger when both lines are pointing in the same direction. In this example, both lines point downwards below 80 or both lines point upwards above 20.

The crossing of the fast line (%K), above the slower line (%D) while in the over-sold zone is positive. A crossing of the slow line (%D), below the fast line (%K) in the over-bought zone is negative. Again, as with the RSI oscillator, the most useful signal to look for with this indicator is divergence, as divergence becomes a leading indicator.

Working only from the stochastic over-bought or over-sold levels can be quite difficult as false signals are often generated when the lines cross negative above the over-bought level, especially when the market is trending, as with EUR/JPY in Figure 4.17. Here the trend dominates, the stochastic is at over-bought levels and both lines did cross negative but were still above the 80 parameter; during this time the market does not immediately move lower. The signal that the market is reversing only becomes efficient when the faster %K line and the slower %D line are both pointing downwards and are both below 80.

Another good example of divergence as a leading indicator is provided in Figure 4.18 overleaf; this is a market that may be due for a correction. The over-bought and over- sold levels are warnings that the market direction might reverse, but this market requires further confirmation. The divergence is useful for indicating where caution should be applied and that a market may experience a correction at some point.

144 Trading and Investing in the Forex Market Using Chart Techniques

(source MetaQuotes Software Corp)

Figure 4.18 EUR/CHF daily chart showing how divergence provides a warning that all is not well with the bullish price action in this market.

In Figure 4.19 opposite, the buy signal generated by the stochastic signal is very straightforward as both lines are pointing upwards from the over-sold region. Once above the 20 parameter, the market becomes increasingly bullish. When both lines are pointing upwards there is a buy signal generated that in this example, would be considered good enough to follow. The candlestick signal, likewise, produces early signals before the stochastic signal occurs. In Figure 4.20 opposite, the stochastic signal is not so straightforward.

Where the technical indicator becomes uncertain, other indicators have to be used to help confirm a signal. In Figure 4.20 opposite, the buy signal generated on 24 March 2008, as the Stochastic indicator moved out of over-sold levels worked well. There had been a hammer and a bullish engulfing candlestick suggesting higher price action to come. After that short-term trend is over, however, the stochastic signal, although signalling divergence, does not stand out that well until the 90-day simple moving average is placed on the chart. This indicator puts the entire recent price action into context revealing where the price is in relation to the long-term averaged price. The 90-day moving average is also very good for observing the conditions of a market. When the market becomes over extended the 90-day moving average attracts the price action back towards it, often seen as market corrections, and when

Applying Confirmation = Confidence Building 145

(source MetaQuotes Software Corp)

Figure 4.19 EUR/CHF weekly chart with the Stochastic indicator.

(source MetaQuotes Software Corp)

Figure 4.20 EUR/CHF chart with the slow Stochastic indicator. The signals are not always clear. The Stochastic indicator in this example produces effective buy signals but the sell signals are not so straightforward.

146 **Trading and Investing in the Forex Market Using Chart Techniques**

the market is pausing or clustering at the average, a move away from the average can be expected. Simply pull up a chart and place the 90-day moving average on the chart and this will become apparent. It is a very useful barometer.

THE MACD OSCILLATOR

Constructed originally by Gerald Appel, the Moving Average Convergence/ Divergence oscillator uses two exponential moving averages of differing time periods. The cross over of the averages generates buy or sell signals. The averages are also plotted against a zero line or centred and have no upper or lower limits as with the RSI or Stochastic indicators. The advantage of a centred oscillator is that market sentiment can be derived from the position of the indicator when compared to the centre line.

When crossing above "0" the market sentiment is positive, below the "0" line and the market sentiment is negative. Convergence of these two averages and moving towards "0" line suggests that the current trend is moving to a pause or is over. Divergence of the two exponential averages, moving away from "0" line, indicates that the short faster average is moving away from the longer slower average and is suggesting a strengthening trend.

For the purposes of the technical procedures used within this book, the MACD-Histogram is applied. The MACD-Histogram, created by Thomas Aspray in 1986, is based on the difference between the averages of the MACD oscillator, and is displayed as a histogram. A change between the two moving averages can be monitored precisely and this identifies early change in market sentiment before the MACD actually produces a cross over signal. This indicator is usually seen at the base of the chart as a histogram that moves above or below the centre line. The very fact that averages are lagging indicators produces a lagging signal; however, measuring the difference between the averages in effect measures the rate of change, the MACD-Histogram becomes a leading indicator based on a lagging indicator's rate of change. Signals are generated from the histogram when it produces divergence and/or crosses the centre line. This is a very useful indicator for signalling a change in market sentiment by simply observing the histogram in relation to the centre line.

This histogram oscillator functions in the following manner. When the MACD crosses "0", it indicates that the shorter more sensitive moving average is crossing over the longer, slower moving average and generates a buy signal or, at least, positive market sentiment and therefore produces an earlier signal.

Market buy signals will be more reliable if the market is trending up and market sell signals will be more effective if the market is trending downwards.

Momentum oscillators are amongst the most useful of all technical indicators and the divergence that these indicators signal is probably the most useful aspect for the technical trader. Using the basic over-bought and over-sold signals, as with the RSI and Stochastic indicators, and observing divergence allows the technical trader to

Applying Confirmation = Confidence Building 147

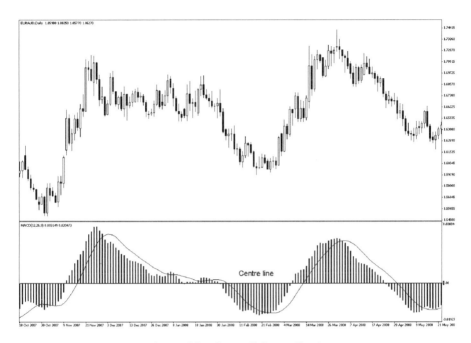

(source MetaQuotes Software Corp)

Figure 4.21 EUR/AUS daily chart showing the MACD oscillator. The histogram produces visual evidence of a change in market sentiment by simply crossing the "0" line.

anticipate moves in the market that may be against the current trend, at least where the technical trader would want to apply caution. If, for example, the market has been moving upwards, perhaps breaking out from some pattern and generally moving in the direction of the overall trend, but divergence appears indicating that the price action may have become irrational, it would be wise to wait for that divergence to play out. In Figure 4.16, divergence can be a good warning! At that level it would be wise not to enter a long position. The bearish engulfing candlestick confirms the divergence that appears on the MACD-Histogram.

The 90-day SMA is useful for the directional bias overall. When the market is difficult to interpret, the 90-day average can show where there is support or resistance and where the market is likely to want to return to at some point. In Figure 4.22 overleaf, the RSI displays good divergence, just as the MACD-Histogram does in Figure 4.23 overleaf, of the same currency. The 10-day channel together with candlestick, however, produced signals to contemplate or trade on a discretionary basis, on each side of the channel. The most challenging scenario in this chart, however, is the 10-day moving average crossing the 90-day moving average. The RSI indicator was in the over-bought zone as the price returned to the inside of the channel and broke below an intermediate trend line as the price broke below the 90-day simple moving average.

(source MetaQuotes Software Corp)

Figure 4.22 AUS/USD daily chart showing the MACD crossing while above "0". Each cross over in a bullish market is followed by positive price action and by the cross over of the 10 and 30-day moving averages, therefore adding confidence to the assumption that the market is changing.

(source MetaQuotes Software Corp)

Figure 4.23 AUS/USD daily chart this time using the 10-day period RSI, 10-day SMA channel against the 90-day SMA.

Applying Confirmation = Confidence Building   149

(source MetaQuotes Software Corp)

Figure 4.24 USD/JPY daily chart with trend line and averages that are confirmed by the MACD-Histogram.

These indicators can be applied to sideways markets for short-term trading, but at some point when the market breaks out the oscillator will already be at the over-bought or over-sold level. The cross over at the "0" line of the MACD-Histogram is used by some technical traders literally as a signal to buy or sell the market. The MACD-Histogram does generate signals effectively at the crossing of the "0" line which should be confirmed by the histogram bars as they increase in the direction of the market price action (be concerned if they do not show signs of market conviction at the crossing of the centre line). The same bars begin to decrease when the market becomes overdone or changes direction. This happens before the MACD-Histogram crosses the "0" line, and some technical traders will begin to enter positions on the first sign of a decline in the histogram bars. Some technical traders will try to enter the market as soon as the histogram bars begin to decrease. The failure to cross the centre line "0" is essentially a signal that the trend will continue. There are no over- bought or over-sold conditions to be measured, but this indicator can work effectively in conjunction with candlestick signals and patterns and other forms of chart analysis. Always consider the candlestick pattern in conjunction with other technical tools especially when divergence appears on the chart as this signal can be very powerful.

150   Trading and Investing in the Forex Market Using Chart Techniques

(source MetaQuotes Software Corp)

Figure 4.25   USD/JPY daily chart. The cross over is followed by negative market sentiment. The averages confirm the market direction.

Another especially good use of the histogram is to identify extreme points where the histogram looks as though it will begin to retreat but is not yet crossed by the nine day ema line. It is early and there is little in the way of confirmation, but it sets up the chart quite well and enables candlesticks to be better judged. In finding such points one is looking for the market price action to have finished its directional move and that the market has found over-bought or over-sold levels. At the point where the histogram fails to make a lower low the technical trader can begin to look for a suitable pivot line to use later as an anchor point and observe the market price action against that level. As with candlesticks they usually produce an early signal and if there is a pivot line to judge the candle against, as in Figure 4.26 opposite a bullish engulfing candlestick that pushes price action above a pivot line, then this is placing market sentiment into context. In this case the context of the pivot line.

The technical trader has a warning not to enter a short position, and instead with some caution enter a long position and monitor this towards the cross over and beyond.

Applying the pivot line establishes an early base line with which to judge the price action confirmed by the candlesticks. Pivot lines are also applied to the first day of the month high and low, as Figure 4.27 opposite demonstrates. The MACD-Histogram is confirming the break lower on each of these months.

Applying Confirmation = Confidence Building

(source MetaQuotes Software Corp)

Figure 4.26 USD/JPY daily chart demonstrating the use of a pivot line that is confirmed, in this case, by the MACD-Histogram failing to make a new low. The pivot line becomes a base line for judging market sentiment indicated by candlesticks.

(source MetaQuotes Software Corp)

Figure 4.27 EUR/CHF daily chart with first day of the month high and low pivot line. The MACD-Histogram is already below the centre line and into negative territory.

CHART ANALYSIS EXERCISE 6

Which technical aspects can you see on the chart in Figure 4.28.

When looking at the daily charts it is always important to look at the size of the candle from the previous session. Study the high, the low and then the close and compare this to the previous session. A series of higher highs and lower highs would suggest that there is buying interest. In Figure 4.28, there are some very visual clues indicating a change of market direction.

(source MetaQuotes Software Corp)

Figure 4.28 GBP/USD daily chart with a slow Stochastic indicator.

CHART ANALYSIS EXERCISE 6 – ANSWERS

On the daily charts the technical areas of importance to a technical trader eventually becomes clear when placed in context. The tendency for technical traders to enter a position too early is caused by looking at individual chart aspects that signal a certain bullish or bearish change but take a few sessions longer before the market actually follows suit. This is quite often the case with Japanese candlesticks, a bullish harami might be followed by a hammer and then a bullish engulfing pattern before the price actually moves higher in the anticipated direction that the bullish harami signalled originally. The market, however, moved higher after the Stochastic indicator produced a buy signal that confirmed the bullish engulfing pattern.

(source MetaQuotes Software Corp)

Figure 4.29 GBP/USD daily chart with double bottom pattern and candlesticks.

CHART ANALYSIS EXERCISE 6 – ANSWERS (CONTINUED)

The RSI indicator likewise set at 10 produces a clear buy signal after the bullish engulfing candlestick appeared and then later divergence producing a second buy signal. As an exit position the RSI would have worked equally well.

(source MetaQuotes Software Corp)

Figure 4.30   GBP/USD daily chart with the RSI indicator.

CHART ANALYSIS EXERCISE 7

Find the following technical aspects in Figure 4.31 on page 156:

1. Engulfing pattern.
2. MACD-Histogram crosses negative into bearish territory.
3. Moving average resistance confirms bearish market direction.
4. Histogram retreats in time to look for a pivot line.
5. Pivot line placed tentatively looking for market reaction around this level.
6. No close above average, still resistance.
7. Pivot line and average hold price action back as candle feels the market, in this case for resistance.
8. Hammer warning of directional change.
9. MACD-Histogram begins to retreat in time to look for a pivot line again.
10. Hammer is possible pivot line.
11. Inverted hammer suggesting higher price action.
12. Bearish engulfing after just one close, the first, above the average in 23 trading sessions.
13. Price action back below the pivot line and slight divergence with the histogram, which is not moving lower with resulting bullish engulfing candle and second close above average.
14. Bullish standard candle closes well above average,
15. Price action above both averages now but the market is uncertain – as reflected by the dojis and the MACD-Histogram which has not crossed the centre line into positive territory,
16. Price back below averages and closes below the pivot line.
17. Potential double bottom forming,
18. MACD-Histogram sloping upwards price action at same level,
19. Bullish engulfing day pushes price action towards the moving average levels and what looks like a triple bottom now forming.
20. Standard positive candle pushes price levels above both averages.
21. Averages cross positive, MACD-Histogram has crossed the centre line into positive territory.

(source MetaQuotes Software Corp)

Figure 4.31   GBP/USD daily chart with MACD-Histogram.

CHART ANALYSIS EXERCISE 7 – ANSWERS

Remember when looking at a chart that the technical aspects of the price have to be found and should fit together, complementing one another. If there are too few clues and the technical aspects are not fitting together then this could be a sign that the price action will continue in the path of least resistance.

Technically, candlesticks represent the market sentiment and display all the insight you require about the day's trading session, yielding first-hand information about the buying and the selling pressure within the market. Adding other technical aspects to the picture is like squaring up the price action and anticipating where the market is not going to go, therefore preparing for the next likely move. The indicators and the averages are there as confirmation tools to help confirm the technical picture.

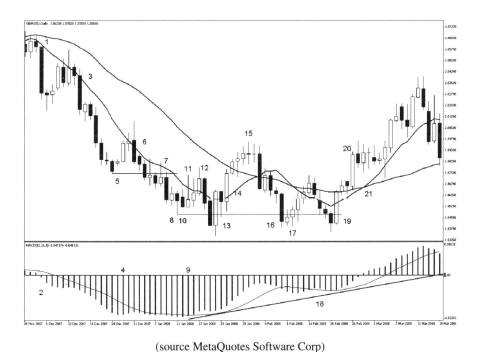

(source MetaQuotes Software Corp)

Figure 4.32 GBP/USD daily chart with MACD-Histogram and technical aspects.

SUMMARY

Moving averages applied to the chart smooth out the price action but the moving average is a lagging indicator. Applying a combination of averages such as the 10, 30 and 90-day averages helps you create a directional bias to the market and a change in market direction when the averages cross negative or positive. Monitoring the daily price action as it reacts to the short-term average is very useful for maintaining the directional bias. The first close below or above the average is a warning of possible change in the market. This is not unlike applying a filter to the close above or below the trend line. The moving average is an area where the bias changes once the market begins to close above or below the average or dips across the average by a certain percentage. Monitoring the 10-day moving average and the 30-day moving average for a bullish or bearish cross over likewise warns of change in the market. When the market price clusters around the averages a directional break can be expected, the longer the price clusters at the average the better the break out will be when it occurs.

Creating averages based on the high and low of the daily price produces channels of support and resistance. These channels filter out irregular market swings. The moving average channel is extremely good for monitoring a trend. A market that is trending upwards tends to remain at and above the upper line with support at the lower line while a market that is trending downwards will remain at and below the lower line finding resistance at the upper line. A change in market direction is expected when the daily price begins to close at the opposite side of the channel. Together with the long-term high and low average a change in market direction can be expected when the averages cross over. The moving average is not very good in range bound markets but the high and low based moving average can still generate good short-term based signals by observing the market for support or resistance at the upper and lower lines.

There are a large number of indicators available in today's computer orientated trading environment and undoubtedly some of these will help to assimilate those areas on charts where the market is providing opportunities, but it is the momentum indicator that is applied in this book because momentum indicators measure the rate of ascent or descent, that is to say, momentum indicators measure the speed of change in market price action and the market price action is what creates the signals on the chart.

There are three methods of applying the momentum indicator to the market price action that work in the markets. The first and most often used technique is direction. Does the momentum indicator confirm the direction of the current market price action? The second technique is to confirm the market as being over bought or over sold and applying caution at these levels. However, one must also consider that a trending market will cause the signal to become over bought or over sold, and that this signal can remain over bought or over sold for many days and weeks. The third and most useful aspect of the momentum indicator is the divergence that these indicators signal, and that divergence becomes a leading indicator. Momentum indicators display the result of the measurement in such a manner that market direction, or over-bought

Applying Confirmation = Confidence Building

or over-sold signals and price divergence, is displayed sufficiently making the task of interpretation very straightforward.

The MACD indicator is seen by market technicians as being one of the most reliable indicators. However, the MACD-Histogram is based on the MACD and is therefore by definition a secondary indicator. The MACD-Histogram is unique for the simplicity of the signal that it generates and for the definable signals. This indicator has stood the test of time and, together with other technical tools, is a great indicator for technical trading.

The momentum indicator helps to time the market for market entry and exit. A bullish engulfing candlestick may suggest higher prices to come, and if the momentum is turning upwards from over-sold levels then that is a good confirmation signal.

Always apply two or three techniques in order to help confirm the technical picture and the more techniques applied the more confidence you will have.

Divergence in the market is one of the best signals that momentum can generate. This is because it becomes a leading indicator, a warning that the market is due for a correction. Always study the markets for divergence and apply a strategy accordingly.

When two or three indicators are confirming a strong signal then technically the market may be providing an opportunity to enter a position. Applying the same technical indicators and techniques set at the same parameters will allow you to see where the market opportunities are. However, one must also observe the strengths and weaknesses of the indicators themselves, with them comes confirmation and confidence in applying these techniques.

5
Entry and Exit = Right or Wrong?

Market entry is a precarious and often unnerving experience. Timing the market for optimal entry is difficult but there are some techniques that make this part of the investment easier. So far, the previous chapters have discussed and demonstrated how to interpret market sentiment and find important areas of support and resistance and how to confirm the opportunities that appear in the markets.

This chapter looks at chart techniques that narrow down or display market price action in such a way that it becomes possible to find optimal levels to enter the market. If the techniques discussed above are pointing to a market that is due for a correction or is ready to move off in a new direction, then entering the market becomes the priority. A position that moves quickly into profit is far superior, both technically and psychology, than one that requires a longer period of time.

In this chapter the following themes are covered:

- Climax volume;
- Pivot lines;
- Core trading pivot areas;
- Highs and lows;
- Japanese candlesticks short-term charts;
- Patterns on short-term charts.

Remember: As with previous chapters, always look at the Japanese candlestick signal in the context of the price level.

CLIMAX VOLUME

Volume displayed at the base of a chart is like having inside information. If a large organisation decided to sell 200 million euros there would only be a few individuals likely to know about this amount of volume preparing to go through the market. Although it is unlikely that you will be able to enter a position parallel to such large orders, the traces will undoubtedly show up on the chart as opportunities worth following.

Volume is a great confirmation tool helping to confirm support or resistance and display it in such a manner that the level becomes a key level which stands out visually on the chart. If a key level is found and the following trading session is accompanied by high volume at that level, this alone adds confidence in the decision that the level is where other traders and investors are buying or selling on the market.

Volume in conjunction with indicators and candlesticks can support the technical set up. High volume confirming candlestick signals, pattern break out points and major support or resistance levels are often decisive on a chart, leaving little alternative. For example, a high volume engulfing candlestick pattern has more conviction when it is seen with higher volume, or a break out from a pattern tends to see a decrease in volume shortly before the break out after which volume should pick up, an important clue. Patterns that are difficult to interpret might be better interpreted by studying the volume activity. Any increase in activity when price breaks out of the pattern is an indication of continuation.

Climax volume is used here to determine when a move in the market is over and when the market may be starting a new direction. A large increase in volume tends to occur at levels where the market buyers or market sellers outweigh the other creating a larger amount of buying or selling pressure than usual.

Figure 5.1 opposite demonstrates quite well how the bullish engulfing candlestick has more conviction when it appears together with high volume. A peak in volume, or climax of volume, can help confirm decisively an area of support or resistance.

Climax volume as a signal for support levels or resistance levels, as in the example shown in Figure 5.2 opposite, demonstrates how useful the confirmation is at the resumption of a trend and during a break out from an ascending triangle, for example. Likewise, a high volume harami candlestick or a high volume bullish engulfing day reveals important clues about market conviction.

Where patterns are difficult to interpret and lead to uncertainty volume can help confirm the pattern during the break out. Applied to a pivot point, volume can be a decisive instrument in gauging the strength of a pivot line, leaving an important level to watch for future reference. A final point of contact is likewise better confirmed when seen with higher volume.

In Figure 5.3 on page 164, the volume climaxes at the point where the market is finding support. At this level the volume is enough to turn the market and although the volume tends to decrease during the upwards trend, it is consistent to begin with

Entry and Exit = Right or Wrong? 163

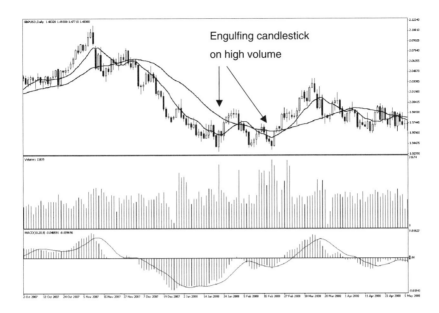

(source MetaQuotes Software Corp)

Figure 5.1 GBP/USD daily chart with volume spikes or climax volume.

(source MetaQuotes Software Corp)

Figure 5.2 EUR/USD daily chart with high volume harami candlestick pattern and high volume engulfing candlestick. When the price action moves lower it attracts buying pressure.

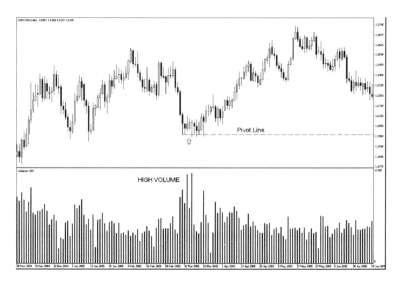

(source MetaQuotes Software Corp)

Figure 5.3 USD/CAD daily chart demonstrating a pivot line with volume which confirms the level.

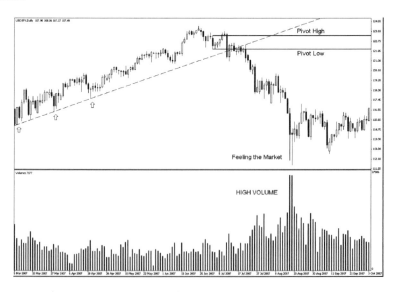

(source MetaQuotes Software Corp)

Figure 5.4 USD/JPY daily chart showing the break lower from the first day of the month pivot high/low. A slight increase in volume during this break out is good confirmation but not nearly as good as the volume that appears later when the market has moved lower and finds major support.

Entry and Exit = Right or Wrong?   165

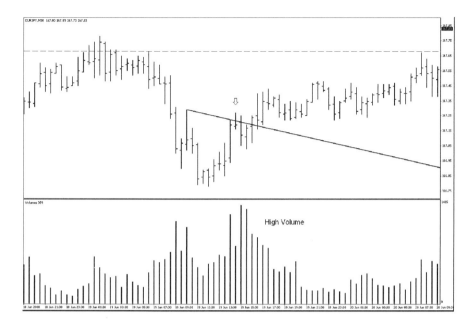

(source MetaQuotes Software Corp)

Figure 5.5 EUR/JPY 15 min. chart displaying high volume levels.

and then drops off creating a kind of divergence between the price action and the level of volume, i.e. buying and selling pressure.

Feeling the market on climax volume is another useful way to confirm a major support level. Observing this type of market action on a daily chart will certainly provide confidence in market timing. The same applies to volume on short-term charts. High volume not only confirms support and resistance levels but also confirms break out areas on short-term charts.

The climax in volume in Figure 5.5 suggests that a line of support has been found and verifies the move that follows. In this example, a level of support has been established and confirmed by the increase in buying pressure. If the market returned to this level on strong volume it would be a sign that the support may be waning. The technical level should already be known and displayed on the chart before the market reaches the level; the increase of volume then confirms this level.

PIVOT LINES AS ENTRY AND EXIT

It is a difficult task to enter a trade in the market at exactly the point where the market moves off, carrying your position into profit. Pivot lines, as has already been demonstrated, can produce areas that narrow down the market to the point where the decisive move occurs. Pivots provide efficient market entry points. If the level is proving significant, as seen by an increase of volume and a range of other technical aspects that support the level, positioning a stop order above or below the pivot line is essentially taking advantage of optimal risk/reward.

One especially good method of looking for confirmation is to apply the level to the shorter time frame and observe the market on an hourly basis as it reacts to the level. As the level holds the point at which the market makes a final touch with that level will becomes apparent, but so does the large increase in volume that should be appearing. Once volume has confirmed the level and the price is seen to have made a final contact with the level, a trade can be entered in the market.

For example, the EUR/USD cross in Figure 5.6 had been range trading between November 2007 and February 2008. After failing twice to break out higher but yet gaining support upon each downside break out attempt, it looked set to move higher. The averages had converged but price action had moved higher towards the pivot line or the pivot line was attracting the price. Also, the momentum indicator was over sold and pointing upwards again.

(source MetaQuotes Software Corp)

Figure 5.6 EUR/USD daily chart with a key pivot line showing how the price rotates around the level as the market pauses during the trend and eventually finds support at the 10 and 30-day averages which propel the price action higher out of the triangle pattern.

Entry and Exit = Right or Wrong? 167

(source MetaQuotes Software Corp)

Figure 5.7 EUR/USD 60 min. chart demonstrating the support from the daily chart where the averages support the price action. The 60 min. chart finds support at the important trend line and intermediate trend line area, but the price is expected to break out of the triangle and continue the trend. This short-term chart is there to find the optimal market entry point.

On 21 February 2008 the price action finally broke through out of its range and failed twice to move higher. The daily candles prior to this break out found support on the long-term 90-day moving average, and the price action had moved back above the 10-day moving average, the stochastic was in over-sold territory and coming back out with both lines crossing positive. There were technical reasons for believing that the EUR/USD would in fact try again to move higher towards the break out line.

On the 60 min. chart it was possible to create a technical set up using the pivot line from the daily chart which would allow a position to be set in the market with a relatively tight stop if the anticipated move higher failed to break out. Figure 5.6 shows how the set up would have looked going forward from the daily to 60 min. chart.

Taking the EUR/USD example in Figure 5.6, the market eventually breaks out and continues the trend higher. By watching the daily chart, by creating a daily technical picture, the higher highs and higher lows that would have been observed after finding support of the base of the pattern. The technical trader would have been prepared for this opportunity.

A strategy would be something like this, looking at Figure 5.7. From the 15th it is possible to create a short-term pivot which, as it happens, turns out to be very useful.

On the 19th price action breaks out above an intermediate trend line and moves up through the short-term pivot line to pause at the long-term pivot line. On the 20th after a volatile day and a test of a trend line price action ended the day higher back above the short-term pivot line – an important clue. On the 21st the price action is definitely back at the long-term pivot line. At this point a buy order is placed in anticipation of the move higher towards the break out line and beyond.

The good part about this short-term technical set up is that the stop order can be placed just below the proven long-term pivot line or just below the short-term pivot line. Either way, the risk is limited against the reward and as it turns out, the stop loss order could have been moved up to the entry level after just a few hours limiting any potential loss if the market failed to make progress. This is just one method of finding market entry levels based on simple pivots and trend lines. It is, of course, part of a plan, that is part of the bigger picture, and it is always important to consider the overall trend when looking at short-term charts. Very often a market will move away from the top very quickly only to return and push higher for a few sessions. A typical example of this is the head and shoulders pattern, where the market tends to return to the neck line. The market tends to return to the last most valid point, touches the level for one final time and then moves away. The opposite applies in a down trend.

Missing the start of a new direction or market trend, however, can be a little disconcerting to some technical traders who like to find the optimal level to enter the market. Finding such opportunities should be the priority of every serious technical trader. Finding opportunities in the market is something that takes practice and patience, but recognising that the market is offering an opportunity can also be quite difficult with the amount of news that often accompanies one-day events. The bearish engulfing day in Figure 5.8 opposite would have been disconcerting for many traders, but for the technical trader the market is trending above a trend line and has recently moved out from a bullish flag scenario. With those two facts alone that bearish engulfing day would become interesting to examine. The question that you would have to ask is, where is the bearish engulfing pattern reversing from?

Quite simply, candlesticks should always be placed into context. If reversal signals are appearing, then try to confirm the level at which they are appearing using other techniques. Find the support or resistance level. If there is no context then the signal may just be a one-day phenomenon.

The 60 min. chart with a daily pivot line drawn on the hourly chart establishes the level where the price is likely to falter. As in Figure 5.9 opposite, technically until the market trades above the high of the bearish engulfing day and closes above it, it is not clear that the market will move higher. However, using the high of the next trading session and the pivot line, it is possible to create a technical set up that allows for a market entry with a minimal loss scenario. The 60 min. chart in Figure 5.9 shows two very important technical aspects. First, the market price action has returned to the pivot line during the very next trading session, secondly there is high volume.

Looking at the market two days after the bearish engulfing candlestick it becomes clear that lower price action attracts buying pressure, this is confirmed by the high

Entry and Exit = Right or Wrong?

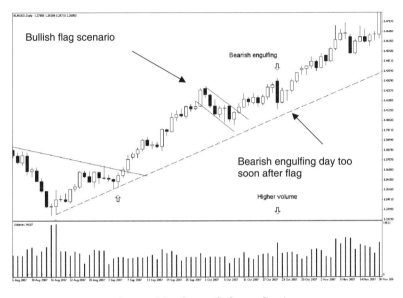

(source MetaQuotes Software Corp)

Figure 5.8 EUR/USD daily chart showing a bull trend with a bearish engulfing day. The bullish flag scenario would suggest that the market has further to go and that the bearish engulfing day is therefore just a one-day sell off that can be turned to the bullish technical trader's advantage.

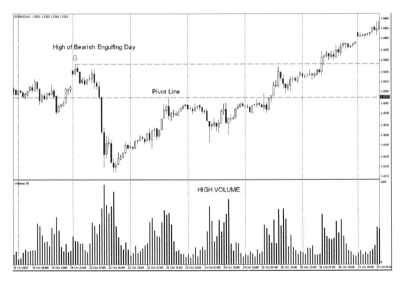

(source MetaQuotes Software Corp)

Figure 5.9 EUR/USD 60 min. chart of a daily bearish engulfing pattern.

levels of volume at that area. On the third day, after the bearish engulfing day, the price action moves higher, the climax volume provided another early signal about market sentiment. At this point a market order to buy could have been positioned at the high of the previous day's session. This is optimal entry because once the market moves above the pivot line, a market stop order can be brought up to the entry point, again this happens relatively quickly and once the price action gets above the high of the bearish engulfing day the market continues higher.

Pivot lines and volume can help enormously in determining areas where the market is turning, where the market is providing an opportunity.

HIGH/LOW/CLOSE AND HIGH/LOW CALCULATED PIVOT LINES

Using the core of the previous day's trading in order to determine market direction during the following sessions is very common amongst day traders, and is still used today by pit traders. It is also very useful for providing entry levels, exit points and for positioning stops. This calculation method is the same as that examined in Chapter 3.

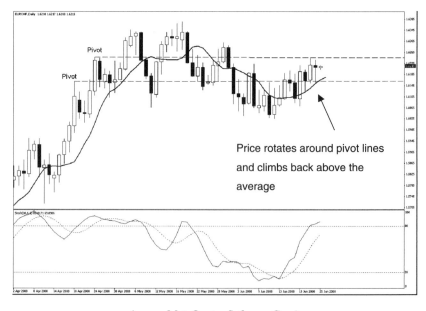

(source MetaQuotes Software Corp)

Figure 5.10 USD/CAD daily chart with a 10-day moving average. The price has been rotating around the pivot line until the average provides a shelf of support. At this point by turning to the short-term chart and finding the core of the day's previous trading, insight into current market sentiment is obtained while the market is at the level. Any uncertainty or change in market sentiment will be displayed first in the movements of the price action on the short-term chart. It is important to refrain from basing a technical view based only on short-term charts.

Entry and Exit = Right or Wrong?

(source MetaQuotes Software Corp)

Figure 5.11 USD/CAD 30 min. chart with a core pivot line.

(source MetaQuotes Software Corp)

Figure 5.12 EUR/CHF 60 min. chart demonstrating a core pivot line which confirms support as the market dips briefly into the area of support where buying pressure increases.

172   Trading and Investing in the Forex Market Using Chart Techniques

The previous day's trading range, that is, the high, the low and the close, are added together and divided by three. This provides the core of the previous day's price action.

This type of core pivot line determines the level at which the market is bullish or bearish. Holding above or below the level creates a bias for market direction which can unfold as the day progresses. This method this is especially good in when applied in conjunction with the other techniques and signals discussed so far and found on daily charts.

Applying the core of the previous trading session to the short-term chart confirms the market price action based on the previous day's trading. Looking for the direction to unfold and the bias to develop can be supported by other techniques. This may also confirm certain candlestick signals on the daily chart. If the previous session was a bullish hammer then the short-term core pivot as support will be that much stronger.

There is no reason why daily technical features cannot be drawn on the shorter time frame, but the short-term chart is likely to see more volatility which can be a little disconcerting, at least in the short term. There is also a danger of becoming too close to the price action when observing only the short-term charts and thus losing the bigger technical picture in the process. Any large organisation that works with the forex markets will be looking at the daily charts. If the position is an investment then it may continue over a long period of time before a position is entirely in the market.

CANDLESTICKS ON SHORT-TERM CHARTS

Whatever type of trading you try to achieve, one thing has to be very clear, you must understand the type of trade that you want to make and the time frame that best suits this method. The opportunities will then present themselves better if the time frame is understood. Likewise, if you prefer to be a buyer, that is, someone who prefers to be long in the markets rather than short, you will have more success if you go through the markets consistently looking for a market that is about to trend upwards or is trending upwards. By being selective you minimise the amount of markets that you have to watch. These methods will allow you to find the optimal market entry and the right conditions, and a trending market will allow you to enter your position and within a short time move into profit. However, if you are not in profit within a relatively short period of time, then something might be wrong with the set up. In Figure 5.13 opposite, EUR/GBP has been trending for many weeks. A bullish engulfing candlestick appears on the daily chart and validates a break out that has reason to remain positive.

The close of the engulfing candlestick is above the 10-day simple moving average and the intermediate trend line. The close of the engulfing pattern has also taken the price back towards the tweezer top of the failed break out, the momentum indicators are pointing downwards and looking negative which might be a slight set back in maintaining an overall positive stance. Looking back over the last 14 sessions, however, the market is still looking very bullish. The low of the bullish engulfing pattern has found support at a level that was recently resistance, another reason

Entry and Exit = Right or Wrong? 173

(source MetaQuotes Software Corp)

Figure 5.13 EUR/GBP daily chart showing a failed break out resulting in a tweezer pattern and later a valid break out resulting in a marabozu type candlestick.

to believe that this market is not about to change direction and that this market is presenting itself with an opportunity to join the trend or add a position that may already be in the market.

The same techniques applied to the daily charts can be applied to the short-term charts. The techniques, however, are more reliable on the daily and weekly charts. In Figure 5.14 overleaf, the one-hour chart clearly shows the engulfing day represented here as many standard positive candlesticks that lead eventually to a key day pivot line that is applied to the chart as soon as the MACD-Histogram begins to retreat! This pivot line creates the bias. The market rotates around the line until support or resistance finally kicks in one way or the other. The market continues to move upwards. Waiting for this requires not only time and patience, but also a suitable entry point. Leaving an order at the high of the engulfing day session would have been one method. However, in this instance it would have required a lengthy stop loss order left in the market which might have been activated during the very next session as the market whipsawed higher, collecting orders, and then moved sharply lower below the 30 SMA activating the stop loss orders before continuing the upwards trend.

The optimal entry point would have been the somewhere above the pivot line with a stop just below, but only after the market had validated the pivot line.

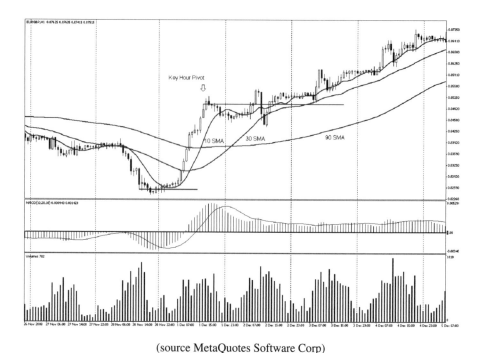

(source MetaQuotes Software Corp)

Figure 5.14 EUR/GBP on the one-hour candlestick chart showing how the break out on the EUR/GBP daily chart looks on the short-term chart.

In the example in Figure 5.14, the market finds support at the 30 hour simple moving average once it is above the pivot line. Buying the market at the 10-hour simple moving average or even better at the 30-hour simple moving average with a stop loss order below the pivot line would have been justified. The day and the stop can be brought up towards the 30-hour simple moving average.

Charts are always easy in hindsight, but the fact remains that these technical scenarios present themselves in the market as opportunities to profit from. They happen frequently, the difficulty is in observing all the markets and having the patience to wait for the optimal entry point to present itself.

PATTERNS ON SHORT-TERM CHARTS

Chart patterns on short-term charts also provide opportunities to enter the market. Looking at the chart in Figure 5.15 opposite. the daily candlestick produced a key day pivot line on 13 November 2008, that is, it placed on the chart only after the MACD-Histogram began to retreat. Clearly the market price action was rotating around the pivot line looking for support or resistance.

Entry and Exit = Right or Wrong? 175

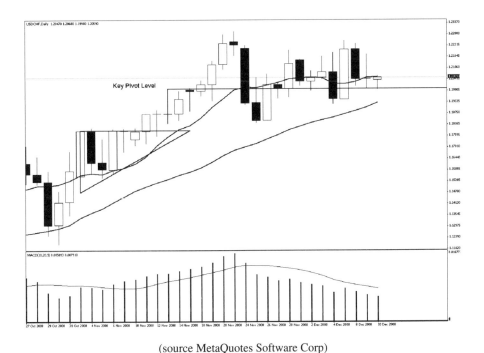

(source MetaQuotes Software Corp)

Figure 5.15 USD/CHF daily candlestick chart demonstrating a key day pivot line at work. The price rotates around the pivot line.

A hourly bar chart will produce the same patterns found on the daily charts. The hourly chart in Figure 5.16 overleaf demonstrates quite clearly how significant patterns can be when found on the short-term charts. This chart also has the key pivot line taken from the daily chart and transferred to the hourly chart. During the trending phase of the market the patterns become quite suitable as a means of buying the market on breaks, but after the short-term inverted head and shoulders pattern the market becomes volatile, experiencing whipsaw type conditions. The pivot line will eventually be the key to finding market direction.

SUMMARY

In this chapter entry and exit methods have been discussed with a focus on volume, pivot lines and the core of the previous trading session. Volume has to come from a reliable source for it to be valid as an instrument by which to judge an area of support or resistance. Large orders going through the market at levels which are already marked out will confirm those levels and provide one with potential entry and or exit points.

(source MetaQuotes Software Corp)

Figure 5.16 EUR/GBP on the one-hour candlestick chart showing how the break out on the EUR/GBP daily chart looks on the one-hour short-term chart.

Pivot lines require confirmation. These levels must be validated before applying them properly as levels to watch for a market entry or market exit. This also applies to the core pivot line taken from the previous trading session. Just because the market is holding at a particular level does not mean that it validates the level as being the line in the sand. As happens with trend lines, the price level in question is best validated after the market has tested the area on at least two occasions.

All of these methods can be applied to market corrections where the concept of buying dips or selling rallies on the daily charts is seen as one of the most frequently used methods for entering the market, either adding to positions or joining a missed opportunity. Applying Fibonacci retracement zones and candlesticks at market corrections can highlight the most suitable areas to look for support or resistance.

Based on the concept of trend lines, pivot lines and Fibonacci retracement zones, the use of short-term charts with volumes and pivot lines and core pivot lines creates strategies through which a sound investment can be initiated with good risk/reward.

Entry and Exit = Right or Wrong?

Slippage is a problem in all markets and will continue to be so, regardless of how efficient the markets are becoming. Using the short-term charts requires great discipline and adherence to the risk area where the stop order should be positioned. Many long-term strategies require that positions are built up to a sizable amount with each entry so planned that the stop loss can be extended to allow for volatility and wild market swings. It is the initial entry that is often difficult and requires patience and good planning.

6
Putting it all together = Practice and Patience

In this chapter the techniques discussed in the previous chapters are pulled together in order to show how it is possible to produce a technical plan. It is a task that allows one to monitor the markets for opportunities worth exploiting. Scouting the charts looking for clues about possible changes or monitoring established positions should be part of the daily routine as a technical trader and investor. If the weekly or daily charts do not signal any opportunities or there is little in the way of conviction in the market, there is little point in trying to force a signal and risk getting caught in a market that is based on hope or uncertainty. Patience is a great virtue, and a protector of wealth! Creating a plan in order to work through the charts is necessary. Setting criteria, as a list, and working through it like a flight plan, is an essential part of being consistent in the undertaking of observing the markets for trade and investment opportunities.

The checklist may look something like this:

Monthly chart, is it trending or range bound?

- Candlestick signal?
- Any chart patterns?
- Where are the support and resistance levels which should be observed?

Weekly chart

- Candlestick signal?
- Any chart patterns?
- Is the market trending or range bound? Where is this in relation to the monthly chart?
- Support and resistance levels?

180   **Trading and Investing in the Forex Market Using Chart Techniques**

Daily chart

- Where is the market in relation to the weekly and monthly charts?
- Are there any clear candlesticks signals?
- Any patterns?
- Where are the support and resistance levels, pivot lines, trend lines and intermediate lines? Do these levels match those on the weekly and monthly chart?
- Where is the price in relation to the support and resistance levels?
- What are the momentum indicators suggesting?

The tools

- Japanese candlesticks;
- Chart patterns;
- The RSI momentum indicator;
- The Stochastic indicator;
- The MACD indicator;
- The moving averages (high/low);
- Pivot lines;
- Fibonacci levels;
- Volume.

FINDING THE TECHNICAL PICTURE

The trend is the most significant and most important starting point in any market and on any chart. Is the market trending? That should be the first and most important factor when looking at markets. If a market is trending where are the levels which one should be watching? If a market is not trending and is range bound how long has the market been range bound and where are the levels for a break out?

In Figure 6.1 opposite, the monthly USD/CHF chart is clearly in a down trend. Placing a trend line on the chart verifies this fact and the downwards trend becomes clearly visible. The market, however, seems to have found an important support level. The monthly candlestick is a bullish engulfing candlestick that has since pushed prices higher in USD/CAD.

Technically on the chart in Figure 6.2 opposite the price action bounced off a projected Fibonacci level at 261.8 % of the extended wave projected down from the break out at 1.3400. The stochastic indicator was over sold. Immediately, there are two very important clues. Switching to the weekly chart, the current state of the market price action has become range bound.

In Figure 6.3 on page 182, since the hammer candlestick formed on the weekly chart, the market price action has pushed higher towards a 50 % Fibonacci retracement zone, although attempts to find buying interest above this level have failed.

Putting it all together = Practice and Patience 181

(source MetaQuotes Software Corp)

Figure 6.1 USD/CAD monthly chart showing the market in a downwards trend with two points of contact at the start of the trend line.

(source MetaQuotes Software Corp)

Figure 6.2 USD/CAD monthly chart with Fibonacci retracement zones.

(source MetaQuotes Software Corp)

Figure 6.3 USD/CAD weekly chart with a clear hammer signal pushing prices up from the Fibonacci level on the monthly chart.

Looking at the daily chart in Figure 6.4 opposite, the current price action has moved below the average and the Stochastic indicator was over sold. Also, the price action failed to hold above the pivot line again. By going through the charts from monthly to daily is it possible to create an overall picture of what the price action is doing or not doing?

1. The monthly chart has found support and traded higher, there is a Fibonacci level at 2.618 % and a large engulfing candlestick = support level.
2. The weekly chart, however, shows that prices have failed to hold above the pivot line and found resistance at the Fibonacci 50 % level = resistance.
3. The daily chart shows that price action has closed below the average and is testing the Fibonacci retracement level = resistance.

The big picture is that USD/CAD seems to have found a major support level at the 0.9050 zone. This level has been tested twice on the daily chart. The daily chart has some technical areas that would be very useful to watch for possible changes in trend and a break out of the current range. By noting the most significant levels it will be possible to anticipate a break out of the range. Placing Fibonacci retracement zones

Putting it all together = Practice and Patience 183

(source MetaQuotes Software Corp)

Figure 6.4 USD/CAD daily chart with potential retracement levels. Prices are closing below the average and have dipped towards the 50 % retracement level so far.

(source MetaQuotes Software Corp)

Figure 6.5 USD/CAD daily chart, the price action eventually finds support at the 61.8 % retracement zone. Note that the key pivot line is holding at this level. When lines meet at the same level that level will have greater significance.

from the most high to the low, there are two areas that become clear immediately: the 50 % level and the 61.8 % level.

The retracement zones were potential targets and areas to watch for support. The price action was trading below the average and the stochastic is still pointing down. Prices look vulnerable to further downside activity. In this instance it would be safer to look for a level to hold as support and then for the price action to target the simple moving average if one of the two Fibonacci levels holds as support. Breaking the time frame down and studying the 60 min. chart would most likely show what, if any, market conviction there is once the price reaches the 50 % or 61.8 % level.

Remember: a market will usually experience a complete retracement if the 61.8 % zone fails to hold the price action.

In Figure 6.6, the 60 min. chart shows how well the market reacts to the support levels from the daily chart. The risk of entering a buy position just above the support level would not outweigh the reward. In this case, the reward looks set to be far greater considering that the monthly and weekly charts are showing that this market has reached a major support level and that the daily chart is now at the all important 61.8 % retracement zone; and where the volume on the 60 min. chart confirms that

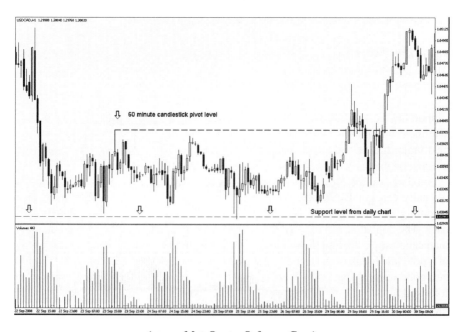

(source MetaQuotes Software Corp)

Figure 6.6 USD/CAD 60 min. chart with volume and a key pivot line and the 61.8 % Fibonacci retracement level from the daily chart. Proves to be good support on the 60 min. chart. Tentative buy positions could be entered here.

Putting it all together = Practice and Patience

(source MetaQuotes Software Corp)

Figure 6.7 USD/JPY daily chart with a 61.8 % Fibonacci retracement after failing to hold. Although the first touch held the price back and closed above the level, the level itself came under pressure resulting in a 100 % retracement.

support of the market. Once the price action responds to the underlying bullish sentiment and moves higher, the daily simple moving average would become the next major hurdle and target. Watch for the price to close above the simple moving average on the daily chart in order to keep the market positive.

Another example of trade ideas based on chart technical analysis can be seen in the daily chart of EUR/AUD cross. The market broke higher after a large bullish engulfing candlestick and once the averages had crossed the market never looked back. The doji at the top of the trend was the turning point. Two days later a hanging man candlestick (feeling the market), closed just on the averages, but was a warning of a potential break of the trend line support. Divergence on the RSI indicator would be a good warning that prices were getting toppy. A day of trading below the averages followed by two closes above the average resulted in a tweezer top. Three days after the tweezer the averages crossed negative. The market never looked back after that.

Remember: it is useful to move down to shorter time frame charts such as the 60 min. chart in order to find the same levels of support and resistance that are on the daily charts. Pivots such as the first hour of the week high and low are good and can greatly improve the directional bias.

186 Trading and Investing in the Forex Market Using Chart Techniques

(source MetaQuotes Software Corp)

Figure 6.8 EUR/AUD daily chart providing an example of finding opportunities by analysing the chart.

(source MetaQuotes Software Corp)

Figure 6.9 USD/JPY daily chart with no technical aspects.

Putting it all together = Practice and Patience

(source MetaQuotes Software Corp)
Figure 6.10 USD/JPY daily chart with some technical features.

By applying the same indicators consistently to the chart opportunities will present themselves and you will be ready when they appear. In being consistent you will also become familiar with the strengths and weaknesses of chart indicators such as the momentum indicator. Being consistent with the same indicators and techniques will generate confidence in your ability to judge the market direction when the right signals are seen.

- Japanese candlesticks;
- Chart patterns;
- The RSI momentum indicator;
- The Stochastic indicator;
- The MACD indicator;
- The moving averages (high/low);
- Pivot lines;
- Fibonacci levels;
- Volume.

188 Trading and Investing in the Forex Market Using Chart Techniques

(source MetaQuotes Software Corp)

Figure 6.11 AUS/USD daily chart with channel moving average and a key day pivot line.

USD/JPY found resistance and the stochastic indicator was at over-bought levels. The pivot line was very valuable in determining the line of resistance and eventually the high of the high/low moving average contained the price action together with a doji evening star candlestick. Prices moved much lower finding support at a previous pivot line and the first Fibonacci level. After seeing the doji close below the high of the moving average a market order could be placed at the pivot line to sell USD/JPY with a stop at the high of the doji, a low risk trade. With practice, this type of scenario will be seen over and over again in the financial markets.

The AUS/USD daily chart in Figure 6.11 suggests that there is no signal either way. The last few sessions had seen volatility pushing the price action back over the pivot line. A clue, however, that this might struggle to move higher is the recent rejection from fresh highs, an area worth watching over the next few sessions.

This chart would be worth observing in a daily watch list. If the price action is seen below the pivot line and the high of the moving average high/low it would be necessary to watch for a candle signal or go down to the 60 min. chart and watch the volume reaction to the pivot line. At some point the technical indicators will line up and multiple indicators pointing to resistance (or support) at the same price zone will provide even more confidence for entering the market. The price action is bullish so watching for support or a break above the high would be necessary.

Having seen the head and shoulders pattern forming on the charts you would have wanted this market in your watch list. Again, patience will have been the key here

Putting it all together = Practice and Patience   189

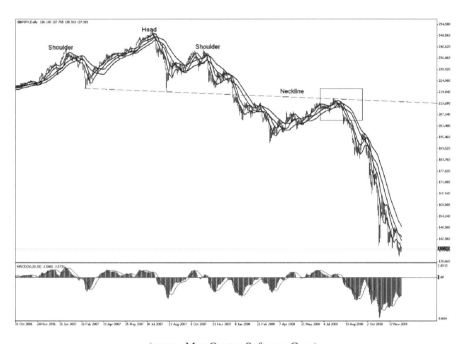

(source MetaQuotes Software Corp)

Figure 6.12 GBP/JPY daily chart zoomed out and showing a classic head and shoulders reversal pattern.

because you would need to wait for the optimal point at which to enter a short position in the market.

In Figure 6.12, the head and shoulders pattern develops a neckline and knowing that many patterns have a base line to which the price returns after the break out has occurred – in this case, a neckline with a head and shoulders pattern – the optimal point of entry would be around the neckline. This would allow for a low risk, high reward investment which, considering the size of the head and shoulders pattern, would last for four or five months. The only challenge here would take the form of staying with the investment, perhaps adding to the position, and not succumbing to taking profits too soon!

By examining the daily chart close up, the market reveals a type of negative engulfing tweezer pattern which appears at the neckline of the head and shoulders pattern. A candlestick pattern appearing at this level is what you would want to see and expect. The neckline is already on the chart and you will have been anticipating the return move. By studying the relationship of the price to the 10-day simple moving average channel it would be assumed, and rightly so, that the price in an upwards trending market tends to remain at or above the high average line, thus waiting for the price action to be below the upper line and then confirming the upper line as resistance. This would be the most suitable way of entering this market. Once the

(source MetaQuotes Software Corp)

Figure 6.13 GBP/JPY daily chart showing a close up view of a return move to the head and shoulders neckline.

upper resistance line has been confirmed as resistance it would be better to move to the hourly chart in order to find a suitable entry point.

The tweezer is a good signal forming at the neckline, but it might be too late to enter at the market at the neckline. The next best position would be to wait for the price to get below the high of the 10-day moving average channel and confirm the upper channel line as resistance.

The hourly chart in Figure 6.14 opposite shows the daily pivot line transferred to the hourly chart and also an intermediate trend line that becomes apparent along the lower highs and at the lows on the hourly candlesticks. Waiting for the break below the lower and shorter intermediate trend line was what many short-term traders would have done. The break out, however, that occurred above the higher trend line corresponds to the simple moving average upper channel line on the daily chart. The market price action at this level presented a very good opportunity to enter the market with a stop at the neckline or just above.

CREATING THE WATCH LIST

Like with most things, it is necessary to have some sort of plan. The more time you devote to your plan the stronger it will be. Creating a list of markets with the same technical set up and going through these at the end of each day will certainly help to

Putting it all together = Practice and Patience   191

(source MetaQuotes Software Corp)

Figure 6.14   GBP/JPY One-hour chart with price.

(source MetaQuotes Software Corp)

Figure 6.15   USD/JPY daily chart showing an example of part of a watch list.

find the right market set up and monitor the markets for signs of change or weakness. It is also very useful to write down the daily charts' technical aspects. This can be done simply by adding a short text to the charts so that they are there in note form and as a reminder.

Creating a plan will help to keep you up to date with technical events, but it will also act like a diary, keeping your observations up to date. Above all, it will force you to develop discipline and become consistent with the techniques until they are second nature, like driving a car.

Creating a plan might look something like this:

USD/JPY Daily Chart – 23/06/08 – Technical Notes

Moved higher throughout the day finding resistance at the Fibonacci 1.382 projection level at 108.06. The market finished the day below the average!
The most suitable key pivot area is at 107.76.
Significantly, the lower pivot of the first hour of the previous week is still proving valid. Resistance is at 108.05.
Support is at the 30-day average area. Currently around 105.77.
This market is looking increasingly negative, having tested resistance levels now on a number of occasions.
Note: It might be worth calculating the core trading area of today's trading on the short-term chart and watching to see if the pivot area can hold the price action tomorrow.
Resistance: 108.20 108.05
Support: 105.77 105.65

Is it worth waiting for the right set up? Certainly the markets present very clear opportunities that have a very good risk/reward ratio. The temptation to try for each and every short-term move will no doubt attract some traders and investors and some will be very successful at this. It is however, extremely tiring and to be at the PC all day requires a great deal of endurance and concentration. Daily and weekly charts therefore eliminate the noise and the problem of getting caught up in each and every market move. It is very wise to be clear about the time frame that suits your investment. Many investments set out to run for the medium to long term only to see the market move back to where the position was entered causing much distress in the process. This is often accompanied by uncertainty resulting from some economic news releases or self-generated fear if the position is large. Disappointment follows from not having taken profits before the market moved against the position. Consequently, traders switch to short-term trading, taking profits as soon they are seen and the long-term strategy is abolished or forgotten. It is, however, the medium-to long-term investment that yields the best profits. This is why finding the optimal

Putting it all together = Practice and Patience   193

entry point is very important for the long-term investment strategy. However, simply deciding on the most suitable time frame and staying with this decision will make trading and investing much easier.

The technical methods of reading a chart that are presented in this book demonstrate that by waiting for the right signal and by being consistent with the indicators and following the signals properly with well planned out stop loss areas, it is possible to join market trends and/or find market turning points. With practice, opportunities will become apparent and good investments may be entered with great skill into a market. A trade placed in the markets from a position of confidence gained from having the right technical set up is an investment which is professional and does not count on luck or hope.

MONEY MANAGEMENT

This is more or less open to the investor to decide. There is a great deal of advice on money management but it is not the duty of this book to tell the reader how to manage money. If the technical aspects of this manual have been understood and especially the section on market entry and exit, then one thing is quite clear: when a market order is placed the chances are that the order will move into profit relatively quickly. If it does not then something is wrong with the point of entry.

Part of the concept of this book is to narrow down the market price action and find areas where there is going to be a reaction. Where the price is set to move off in the anticipated direction within a relatively short period of time but stop loss orders are still difficult to position, especially when the order is of considerable size, it is preferable to categorise the stop loss in the order of the investment criteria. Strictly speaking, many traders who trade sizable positions will not remain in the market for more than ten pips, often less, if the market is moving against them. If the funds are sizable and the investment is placed in the market with the assumption that the market is about to continue trending or begin a new trend, then a stop loss relative to the size of the potential reward must be calculated. As Figure 1.1, in Chapter 1, demonstrates, if the move is expected to be substantial based on the similar criteria which suggested that EUR/JPY would decline, then placing a stop loss order at 150 points above the weekly hanging man would have been very good risk reward as the position could quite easily have been added to once in profit and the stop loss brought down to below the hanging man.

The Forex market can experience very volatile days and on such days a stop loss of 30 pips is not going to be adequate. However, under normal market conditions the stop loss level might be around 25 points behind the most suitable support or resistance level, depending, of course, on the technical set up. If, for example, a pivot line that has been proven to be valid is 33 pips away from the market entry then the stop loss might be 36 pips behind the market entry. It is important to decide what you are prepared to risk according to each trade and the technical arrangement at hand.

If a market investment is to be added continuously to a position over a period of weeks, then each stop loss may be in accordance with the accumulated profit as well as the technical entry point! Another important factor is the size of the position. If the position is large the stop loss may have to be very tight. On the other hand, if a position is small then having a stop loss set at 50 pips behind the entry may be adequate and if the potential win is 450 pips then what is a risk of 50 pips in comparison. For this reason money management is the prerogative of each individual trader and investor. If a trader believes that the technical set up has the potential to realise 450 pips then a 50 pip stop level is okay. Obviously 100 pip stop loss for a gain of only 10 pips is not good money management. Whatever is the best way, nothing compensates for getting out of a bad trade early!

SUMMARY

Creating a plan and developing a strategy based on the plan is an essential part of trading and investing. Having no plan is like getting into a car and driving off down the road with no idea about where you are heading or where you will end up!

The method of creating a plan is very different to actually trading the markets. However, using the daily chart and observing signals and finding the areas where the market is expected to falter after an upwards trend or find support during a downward trend is prejudging the market for an early sign of change, knowing essentially what to do if the market reacts as expected.

Where there is change there is opportunity. Finding these opportunities not only requires careful observation in a consistent manner and good planning, but also a great deal of discipline in order to carry out the plan. It may take two or three attempts before a position is adequately in the market. Nothing is more frustrating than to see a position move 100 pips into profit only to return to the point of entry resulting in the position being stopped out. It is the daily signals that show markets moving off, pausing and consolidating and trending again. These are the signals that are found again and again in the financial markets and provide the necessary proof that the markets do change direction and that they do move upwards and downwards for long periods.

Range bound markets can be stressful and lead to poor performance and for this reason it is necessary to become familiar with the techniques discussed in the previous chapters and with pivot lines where observing the price action for a final touch can be decisive in the final moments of the beginning of a trend or continuation in a trend. This would also apply to false break outs and watching for the next attempt at breaking out.

A WORD ON FILTERS

Many professional technicians apply filters to the markets in order to generate a valid signal. One method is to look for a Friday close beyond a certain level or above the

Putting it all together = Practice and Patience

(source MetaQuotes Software Corp)

Figure 6.16 USD/JPY daily chart showing the 118.00 level as being pivotal. The size of a candle's body above the level in question can yield important clues about the market's reaction at that level. Closing just above the level is not as good as an entire range above the level.

averages in order to see where the week's trading will close. Another method is to watch the daily close above or below the averages. As with all methods, however, it is necessary to find a set up that is suitable to your style and then test how often the filter of a daily close has proven reliable. It may be that two or three closes are necessary at or beyond the level in question or perhaps a certain percentage above or below a level is necessary so as to validate a signal. This is something that has to be researched for each market. In the example in Figure 6.12, the averages cross negative with the long-term average becoming good resistance. The 188.00 level, however, never saw more than one daily close above that level until prices broke higher on 15 December.

A WORD ON RECOMMENDATIONS

Below is a picture of a rabbit. One particular problem with the financial markets is that, owing to the size of the industry, there are an awful lot of recommendations available. Now, whether by design or by chance, recommendations can be so disconcerting to the technical trader that the technical picture becomes distorted; is the rabbit really a rabbit, or is it a duck like others are saying it is?

Exhibit 6.1 Rabbit or duck?

A chart displaying a hammer candlestick that has pushed prices higher above the averages and has had three consecutive closes at a point beyond technical levels and looks set to push the price higher still further, or a bullish asymmetrical triangle that looks set to break higher, loses its strength as a signal because a number of so called experts are saying that the market is likely to move lower based on some fundamental reason. It is usually enough for uncertainty to set in, the element of doubt. Is it a bullish signal or not, perhaps the market will go down, perhaps, after all, it is a duck and not a rabbit!

Charting is objective as long as the technical aspects are seen for what they are signalling; a technically based investment should not rely on recommendations. A technical trader who cannot push the buy or sell button must decide whether it is not better to do something else in life! Any type of risk needs a strategy; if the strategy is sound then the technical trade should have a higher possibility of being correct. Charts do not lie, only the people that do not use them!

FINAL WORD

If you have read this book and understood each of the techniques presented here, then you will also acknowledge the fact that chart analysis involves a great deal of hard work and patience. Examining each and every indicator in relation to market price and checking the averages and looking for lines, then confirming the signals with support or resistance levels or resolving a potential pattern requires stamina and discipline. Above all, waiting for an opportunity to present itself requires a great deal of patience. If a market has reacted with a neckline or a base line it may touch that line and immediately reverse direction, the price may also take weeks of clustering at a certain level before finally moving out into a new direction. Applying the techniques discussed in this book will assist decisively in maintaining an edge in the financial markets.

Technical analysis is not perfect but it offers a unique way to enter and monitor positions in the market. However, the previous chapters have demonstrated that

Putting it all together = Practice and Patience

patterns and candlestick signals exist in the markets and that by training the eye to find these signals, together with important price levels, support and resistance areas, it is possible to create a good overall picture of market direction. Through studying candlesticks together with other techniques it is possible to read the sentiment of the market and identify a change in market sentiment at an early stage and act accordingly. The point of this book is to help you learn to see the signals, then act on those signals. If, however, you apply the techniques as shown in this book you will see that the market has levels where it is moving freely in one direction and areas where the price becomes stagnant. The right technical set up will find markets that are ready to move off and markets that are not going to do much. As long as the technical tools remain consistent these techniques will lead you to create sound and disciplined investment strategies.

Practice makes perfect. Never has a statement held so much truth as with charting the financial markets. As with any rewarding undertaking the amount of practice will be the key to a successful result. Today it is possible to download software and practice chart techniques before opening a real account. This is a great advantage for any beginner or professional alike and is highly recommended before committing real money to the markets.

Appendix

Currency option: Option contract that gives the right to buy or sell a currency with another currency at a specified exchange rate during a specified period. This category also includes exotic foreign exchange options such as average rate options and barrier options.

Currency swap: contract which commits two counterparties to exchange streams of interest payments in different currencies for an agreed period of time and usually to exchange principal amounts in different currencies at a pre-agreed exchange rate at maturity.

Foreign exchange swap: transaction which involves the actual exchange of two currencies (principal amount only) on a specific date at a rate agreed at the time of the conclusion of the contract (the short leg), and a reverse exchange of the same two currencies at a date further in the future at a rate (generally different from the rate applied to the short leg) agreed at the time of the contract (the long leg).

Forward rate agreement (FRA): interest rate forward contract in which the rate to be paid or received on a specific obligation for a set period of time, beginning at some time in the future, is determined at contract initiation.

Instruments

The definitions used for traditional foreign exchange market instruments and OTC derivatives market instruments are the following:

Interest rate option: option contract that gives the right to pay or receive a specific interest rate on a predetermined principal for a set period of time.

Interest rate swap: agreement to exchange periodic payments related to interest rates on a single currency; can be fixed for floating, or floating for floating based on different indices. This group includes those swaps whose notional principal is amortised according to a fixed schedule independent of interest rates.

Outright forward: transaction involving the exchange of two currencies at a rate agreed on the date of the contract for value or delivery (cash settlement) at some time in the future (more than two business days later). This category also includes forward foreign exchange agreement transactions (FXA), non-deliverable forwards and other forward contracts for differences.

Spot transaction: single outright transaction involving the exchange of two currencies at a rate agreed on the date of the contract for value or delivery (cash settlement) within two business days.

Further Reading

Appel, G. (1985) *The Moving Average Convergence–Divergence Trading Method*, W&A Publishing.
Aspray, T. (1989) Individual Stocks and MACD, *Technical Analysis of Stocks & Commodities*, **7**(2), p56–61.
Fisher, M. (2002) *The Logical Trader*, John Wiley & Sons, Inc.
Lefèvre, E. (1994) *Reminiscences of a Stock Operator*, John Wiley & Sons, Inc.
Murphy, J.J. (1999) *Technical Analysis of the Financial Markets*, New York Institute of Finance.
Nison, S. (2001) *Japanese Candlestick Charting Techniques*, New York Institute of Finance.
Schwager, J. (1992) *The New Market Wizards*, John Wiley & Sons, Inc.
Shimizu, S. (1990) *The Japanese Chart of Charts*, Tokyo Futures Trading Publishing Co.
Sperandeo, V. (1993) *Methods of a Wall Street Master*, John Wiley & Sons, Inc.

Useful Websites

http://www..FXStreet.Com

Index

Appel, Gerald 146
ascending triangles, bear symmetrical
    triangle continuation patterns 57, 62
Aspray, Thomas 146
AUS/CAD 7, 19, 31, 40, 48
AUS/USD 15, 33, 37, 39, 49, 55, 58, 64, 75,
    97–100, 103, 118, 122–3, 126, 141,
    142, 148, 188
average rate options, definition 199

back tests
    concepts 3, 14, 84, 127–8, 142–3
    confirmations 84, 127–8, 142–3
bar charts, Japanese candlesticks 9–10,
    175–7
barrier options, definition 199
bear flags continuation patterns
    concepts 54, 56, 57, 81–3
    definition 54, 57
bear markets 3–7, 9–11, 20–32, 34, 36, 37,
    38–9, 43, 45, 49–51, 54, 56, 57, 59, 65,
    68, 73–4, 81–3, 86–7, 92, 99–100,
    120–4, 153–9, 168–70, 182–4, 186–9
bear pennant continuation patterns, concepts
    57, 59
bear rising wedge continuation patterns,
    concepts 65, 68
bear symmetrical triangle continuation
    patterns
    concepts 57, 61–3
    definition 57
bearish belt-hold line candlesticks
    concepts 13, 14, 28–9, 30, 34, 36, 99–100

definition 14, 28
bearish broadening reversal patterns
    see also broadening. . .
    concepts 80
bearish closing bozu candlesticks
    concepts 13, 14, 32, 33, 41, 99–100
    definition 14, 32
bearish engulfing candlesticks
    concepts 9–10, 34, 36, 37, 38–9, 43, 45,
      49–51, 68, 73–4, 99–100, 120–4,
      155–9, 168–70, 182–4, 186–9
    definition 34
    entry/exit issues 168–70, 182–4, 186–9
bearish head and shoulder reversal patterns
    concepts 69–70, 188–90
    definition 69
bearish 'V' bottom reversal patterns
    see also 'V' reversal patterns
    concepts 76–7, 79
    definition 77
black Japanese candlesticks, concepts 8–52
bottoms 20, 28
break outs 2, 5–7, 25, 53–84, 88–99, 101–2,
    106–7, 133–9, 166–7, 172–7, 180–97
    concepts 83–4, 88–99, 101–2, 133–9,
      166–7, 172–7, 180–97
    false break outs 83–4, 95–9, 102–3, 109,
      118–19, 121–4, 135–9, 166–7, 172–3,
      180–2
    strategies 83–4, 167–8
broadening top and bottom reversal patterns
    concepts 77, 80–3
    definition 77

Index

bull falling wedge continuation patterns
concepts 63–4, 84
definition 63
bull flags continuation patterns
concepts 54–5, 120–4, 169
definition 54
bull markets 2, 3, 9–11, 14, 20–32, 35, 41,
43, 45, 47–8, 49–51, 54–5, 57, 58, 60,
65, 73, 75, 77, 80–3, 86–7, 93–4,
99–100, 120–4, 137–9, 144–5, 148,
150–1, 153–9, 162–3, 169, 172–3,
180–1, 182–4, 185–9
bull pennant continuation patterns
concepts 57, 58
definition 57
bull rising wedge continuation patterns
concepts 65, 82–3
definition 65
bull symmetrical triangle continuation
patterns
concepts 57, 60, 120–4, 196
definition 57
bullish belt-hold line candlesticks
concepts 13, 14, 24, 27, 30, 41, 49–51,
99–100
definition 14, 24
bullish broadening reversal patterns
see also broadening. . .
concepts 80
bullish closing bozu candlesticks
concepts 13, 14, 28, 31, 32, 41, 99–100
definition 14, 28
bullish engulfing candlesticks 9–10, 23, 32,
35, 41, 43, 45, 47–8, 49–51, 60, 65, 73,
75, 99–100, 122–4, 137–9, 144–5,
150–1, 153–9, 162–3, 172–3, 180–1,
182–4, 185–9
concepts 9–10, 23, 32, 41, 43, 45, 47–8,
122–4, 137–9, 144–5, 150–1, 153–9,
162–3, 172–3, 180–1, 182–4, 185–9
definition 32
entry/exit issues 162–3, 172–3, 182–4,
185–9
bullish head and shoulders reversal patterns
concepts 67–70, 188–90
definition 67
bullish 'V' top reversal patterns

see also 'V' reversal patterns
concepts 76–7, 78
definition 77
buying 2–3, 7, 8–9, 85–124, 140–59,
161–77, 179–97
see also entry. . .; shadows

calculated pivot lines, concepts 109–10,
170–7
candlesticks
see also individual candlesticks;
Japanese. . .
concepts 1–52
types 2, 8–14
cash settlements, concepts 200
central bank statements 77
channels
see also trend lines
concepts 90–5, 132–9, 158–9
moving averages 132–9, 158–9, 188–97
potential targets 92–3
uses 92–4, 188–97
chart analysis
see also technical analysis
concepts 1–52, 124, 125–59, 162–5,
179–97
confirmations 125–59, 162–5, 179–97
definition 2
final word 196–7
multiple techniques 124, 152–9
overview of the book 1–3, 196–7
patience 179–80, 196–7
practical applications 3, 179–97
recommendations 195–6
software downloads 197
uses 2, 125–59, 162–5, 179–97
watch lists 190–7
climax volumes
concepts 3, 161–5, 175–7,
180–97
entry/exit issues 161–5, 175–7, 180–97
close representation
concepts 8–52, 116–19, 126–7, 152–9,
170–7, 194–5
entry/exit issues 170–7
filters 194–5
uses 52, 116–19, 126–7, 152–9, 170–7

Index

colours of Japanese candlesticks 8–9
confidence-building tools, confirmations 125–59, 162–5, 180–97
confirmations
  back tests 84, 127–8, 142–3
  concepts 3, 20, 34, 38, 43, 52, 54, 57, 84, 86, 125–59, 162–77, 196–7
  confidence-building tools 125–59, 162–5, 180–97
  critique 158–9, 196–7
  entry/exit issues 162–77
  MACD-Histogram 104, 125, 146–59, 173–5, 180–97
  momentum indicators 3, 125, 139–59, 180–97
  moving averages 3, 4–7, 50–2, 125–59, 180–97
  over-bought conditions 3, 5–7, 140–59, 182–97
  over-sold conditions 3, 140–59, 167–8, 182–97
  RSI oscillator 125, 140–2, 147–8, 154–9, 180–97
  stochastic oscillator 5–7, 125, 141–6, 152–9, 180–97
  volumes 162–5, 175–7, 180–97
consolidations 10–14, 24–5, 84, 85–124
continuation patterns
  see also individual patterns; patterns; pauses
  concepts 53–67, 83–4
  critique 83–4
  timescales 84
  uses 83–4
convergence 146–59
  see also divergence; MACD-Histogram
corrections 86–7, 115–17, 124
cross overs, moving averages 129–59
currency options
  see also average rate. . .; barrier. . .
  definition 199
currency swaps, definition 199

daily charts 9–15, 18, 22–42, 47–9, 51, 55–6, 58–9, 61–6, 68–78, 80, 82, 87, 89, 92–4, 97–8, 100–23, 128–31, 135, 138–44, 147–57, 163–75, 180–97

see also individual currencies
pivot lines 100–9, 180–97
practical applications 180–97
uses 50, 51, 180–97
dark cloud cover candlesticks
  concepts 34, 38–9, 45, 104, 120–4
  definition 34, 38
  pivot lines 104
descending triangles, bear symmetrical triangle continuation patterns 63
diamond reversal patterns, concepts 67
direction uses
  momentum indicators 140–59, 180–97
  moving averages 129–39, 147–8, 158–9, 180–97
  pivot lines 99–100, 180–97
distortions 195–6
divergence 3, 127–39, 140–59, 185–97
  see also MACD-Histogram; momentum indicators
doji cross candlesticks
  concepts 13, 14–16, 49–51, 107–10, 121–4, 126, 155–9, 185–97
  definition 14–16
  dragonfly doji candlesticks 16
  gravestone doji candlesticks 16
doji evening star candlesticks 43, 45, 60, 187–9
  concepts 43, 45, 187–9
  definition 43
doji morning star candlesticks
  concepts 43, 46
  definition 43
double bottom reversal patterns
  concepts 53, 69, 72, 75–6, 111–12, 122–4, 138–9, 155–9
  definition 72
double moving averages
  see also moving averages
  concepts 125, 127–39
double signals, Japanese candlesticks 32–52
double top reversal patterns
  concepts 53, 69, 72, 74, 75, 81–3
  definition 72
dragonfly doji candlesticks 16
ducks, rabbits 195–6

Egyptian architecture, Fibonacci ratios
110–11
emotional responses 2
entry levels
concepts 2, 3, 153–9, 161–77, 179–97
confirmations 162–77
pivot lines 161–77, 179–97
short-term charts 161–2, 167–8, 172–7,
184–97
volumes 161–5, 175–7, 180–97
equilibrium in markets 79
EUR/AUS 147, 185–6
EUR/CHF 59, 81, 99, 111, 144–5, 151, 171
EUR/GBP 9–12, 30, 62, 80, 87, 172–6
EUR/JPY 3–7, 22, 47, 51–2, 109, 115,
117–19, 128, 143, 165, 193–4
EUR/USD 45, 74, 82, 102, 104–6, 114, 120,
127–8, 130, 141, 163, 166–9
exit levels
concepts 2, 3, 161–77, 179–97
confirmations 162–77
pivot lines 161–77, 179–97
short-term charts 161–2, 167–8, 172–7,
184–97
volumes 161–5, 175–7, 180–97
exotic foreign exchange options
see also average rate. . .; barrier. . .
concepts 199
expert opinions 2, 195–6
exponentially weighted moving averages
128–9

false break outs 83–4, 95–9, 102–3, 109,
118–19, 121–4, 135–9, 166–7, 172–3,
180–2
fear responses 2
Fibonacci levels
concepts 85–6, 110–19, 124, 127–8,
138–9, 176–7, 180–97
definition 110, 124
hammer candlesticks 112, 180–2
historical background 110–11
Japanese candlesticks 116–17, 138–9,
176–7, 180–97
projection levels 111–19
retracement levels 111–19, 138–9, 176–7,
180–97

uses 111–17, 124, 127–8, 180–97
filters
close 194–5
concepts 88–90, 96–110, 124, 126–7,
194–7
methods 194–5
final word on chart analysis 196–7
financial instruments
see also individual instruments
definitions 199–200
first trading days of the month,
predetermined pivot lines 104–9
fixed legs, interest rate swaps 199–200
flag poles 54–7, 81
see also bear. . .; bull. . .
floating legs, interest rate swaps 199–200
foreign exchange swaps
concepts 199
definition 199
forex markets 86–7, 110–24, 126–59,
193–7
see also individual currencies
forward foreign exchange agreement
transactions (FXAs) 200
forward rate agreements (FRAs), definition
199
fundamental analysis 1, 2, 86
FXAs see forward foreign exchange
agreement transactions

GBP/JPY 46, 68, 91, 112, 189–91
GBP/USD 25, 26, 27, 29, 35, 36, 66, 89, 95,
135, 138–9, 152, 153–4, 156–7, 163
gold markets 60, 113–14
Golden ratio
see also Fibonacci levels
concepts 110–11, 124
gravestone doji candlesticks 16
greed responses 2
Greek architecture, Fibonacci ratios 110–11

hammer candlesticks
concepts 9–10, 13, 14, 16–20, 24, 41,
47–8, 49–51, 68, 79, 89, 100–2, 112,
120–4, 126, 134, 137–9, 144–5, 153–4,
155–9, 180–2, 196
definition 14, 16

Index 207

Fibonacci levels 112, 180–2
pivot lines 100–2, 155–9
hanging man candlesticks 3–7, 13, 14, 20–1,
39, 49–52, 55, 72, 78, 120–4, 185–6
concepts 3–7, 13, 14, 20–1, 39, 49–52, 72,
120–4, 185–6
definition 14, 20
harami bottom candlesticks
concepts 43, 44, 92, 96–100, 118–19,
122–4, 138–9, 153–4, 163
definition 43
harami candlesticks 12–13, 38, 43, 44,
46–8, 52, 58, 64, 65, 71, 75, 92,
96–100, 118–19, 122–4, 138–9, 153–4,
163
harami top candlesticks
concepts 38, 42, 44, 92, 96–100, 118–19,
122–4, 138–9, 153–4, 163
definition 38
head and shoulders patterns
see also bearish...; bullish...; inverted...
concepts 53, 66, 67–70, 168–9, 188–90
higher highs 86–90, 126–7, 152–9
higher lows 86–90, 126–7
highs 5–7, 8–52, 86–90, 99–100, 104–9,
117–19, 125, 126–9, 132–9, 152–9,
161–2, 170–7
entry/exit issues 161–2, 170–7
higher highs 86–90, 126–7, 152–9
moving average high and low indicator
125, 132–9, 158–9, 180–97
predetermined pivot highs and lows 104–9
uses 52, 170–7
histograms, MACD-Histogram 104, 125,
146–59, 173–5, 180–97
Homma, Munehisa (Sokyu Honma) 7–8
Honma, Sokyu (Munehisa Homma) 7–8
hope responses 2
hourly charts, uses 50

instruments
see also individual instruments
definitions 199–200
interest payments 199–200
see also currency swaps; forward rate
agreements
interest rate options, definition 199

interest rate swaps, definition 199–200
intermediate trend lines 85–6, 95–8, 99–100,
117–19, 120–4, 135–9, 147–8, 167,
172–3, 180–97
see also trend lines
concepts 95–8, 99–100, 120–4, 167,
172–3, 180–97
internal trend lines
see also trend lines
concepts 96, 99, 122–4
Internet 2
inverted hammer candlesticks
concepts 13, 14, 20, 23, 45, 47–8, 155–9
definition 14, 20
inverted head and shoulders continuation
patterns
concepts 66, 175–7
definition 66

Japanese candlesticks 1–3, 7–52, 84, 88–90,
116–19, 126, 149–59, 161–77, 179–97
see also individual candlesticks
bar charts 9–10, 175–7
colours 8–9
concepts 7–52, 84, 85–6, 88–90, 126,
149–52, 157–9, 161–77, 179–97
critique 10–11, 50–2, 84, 85–6
definition 8
double signals 32–52
entry/exit issues 161–77, 179–97
Fibonacci levels 116–17, 138–9, 176–7,
180–97
historical background 7–8
MACD-Histogram 149–51, 173–5,
180–97
market sentiments 8–9, 50–2, 85–6, 92–3,
149–51, 157–9, 161–77, 179–97
misinterpretations 10–11
open/high/low/close representation 8–52,
116–19, 126–7, 152–9, 170–7
pivot lines 100–1, 124, 150–1, 179–97
short-term charts 172–7, 184–97
signals 1–52, 85–6, 162–77, 179–97
single signals 7–32
types 2, 11–14
uses 8–10, 50–2, 84, 85–6, 88–90,
149–59, 179–97

key day pivot lines 99–103, 122–4, 171–7, 184–97
  see also pivot lines

Lane, George 141–2
Lefèvre, Edwin 1
Leonardo of Pisa 110
linear weighted moving averages 128–9
long legs, foreign exchange swaps 199
long-term markets 50–2, 77, 90–1, 93–4, 96–9, 114–15, 128–39, 167–8
long-term time horizons, trend lines 50–2, 77, 90–1, 93–4, 96–9, 114–15, 128–39, 167–8
lower highs 86–90, 152–9
lower lows 86–90
lows 8–52, 86–90, 99–100, 104–9, 117–19, 125, 126–9, 132–9, 152–9, 161–2, 170–7, 180–97
  entry/exit issues 161–2, 170–7
  higher lows 86–90, 126–7
  lower highs 86–90, 152–9
  moving average high and low indicator 125, 132–9, 158–9, 180–97
  predetermined pivot highs and lows 104–9
  uses 52, 170–7

'M' patterns *see* triple. . .
MACD-Histogram
  concepts 104, 125, 146–59, 173–5, 180–97
  critique 159
  definition 146–7, 159
  historical background 146
  Japanese candlesticks 149–51, 173–5, 180–97
  pivot lines 104, 173–5
  uses 146–7, 159, 173–5, 180–97
marabozu candlesticks
  concepts 13, 14, 16–18, 28, 47–8, 49–51, 99–100, 106–7, 119, 122–4, 173
  definition 14, 16
  pivot lines 106–7
market angle gradient, trend lines 94–5
market instruments 199–200
  see also individual instruments
market sentiments 8–9, 85–6, 92–3, 125–59, 161–77, 179–97

medium-term time horizons, trend lines 90
momentum indicators
  see also MACD. . .; RSI. . .; stochastic. . .
  concepts 3, 125, 139–59, 180–97
  definition 139–40
  direction uses 140–59, 180–97
  over-bought/over-sold issues 140–59, 167–8, 182–97
  uses 3, 125, 139–41, 146–7, 158–9, 180–97
money management, concepts 193–7
monthly charts
  see also individual currencies
  practical applications 179–97
  uses 50, 179–97
moving averages
  see also MACD-Histogram
  calculations 127–8, 170–7
  channels 132–9, 158–9, 188–97
  concepts 3, 4–7, 50–2, 125–59, 180–97
  critique 128–9, 158–9
  cross overs 129–59
  definitions 125–6
  direction uses 129–39, 147–8, 158–9, 180–97
  high and low indicator 125, 132–9, 158–9, 180–97
  support and resistance levels 127–39, 155–9, 180–97
  timescales 127–31, 173–7
  types 125, 127–9
  uses 125–33, 158–9, 180–97
multiple techniques 124, 152–9

negative cross overs, moving averages 129–31, 155–9
news-related incidents 77, 86–7, 93–4
Non Farm Payrolls 86–7
non-deliverable forwards 200

open representation
  Japanese candlesticks 8–52, 116–19
  uses 52, 116–19, 127–9
opportunities
  concepts 1–3, 53–84, 85–6, 124, 159, 161–77, 179–97
  patterns 53–84, 85–6, 124, 161–77, 179–97

Index

risk/reward ratios 192–3, 196
watch lists 190–7
options
  see also currency. . .; interest rate. . .
  concepts 199–200
OTC derivatives 199–200
outright forwards, definition 200
over-bought conditions 3, 5–7, 140–59, 182–97
over-sold conditions 3, 140–59, 167–8, 182–97
overview of the book 1–3, 196–7

patience 179–80, 196–7
patterns
  see also individual patterns
  concepts 1–3, 53–84, 85–6, 120–4, 161–77, 179–97
  continuation patterns 53–67, 83–4, 120–4
  critique 83–4, 85–6, 124
  entry/exit issues 161–2, 175–7
  opportunities 53–84, 85–6, 124, 179–97
  reversal patterns 2, 28, 32, 53–4, 66, 67–84, 86–124, 138–9, 155–9
  short-term charts 174–7, 184–97
  strategies 83–4, 161–77, 179–97
  timescales 84
  uses 83–4, 85–6, 179–97
pauses 2, 24, 38, 42, 84
  see also continuation patterns
perfect markets 86
piercing candlesticks
  concepts 9–10, 34, 37, 39, 117–19, 120–4
  definition 34
pivot lines
  calculated lines 109–10, 170–7
  concepts 2–3, 7, 16–18, 52, 66, 75, 85–6, 96–110, 115–17, 124, 137–9, 150–1, 155–9, 161–77, 180–97
  daily charts 100–9, 180–97
  dark cloud cover candlesticks 104
  definition 96, 99
  entry/exit issues 161–77, 179–97
  general rules 100–1
  hammer candlesticks 100–2, 155–9
  Japanese candlesticks 100–1, 124, 150–1, 179–97

key day pivot lines 99–103, 122–4, 171–7, 184–97
MACD-Histogram 104, 173–5
marabozu candlesticks 106–7
market directions 99–100, 180–97
positioning practices 100–1
predetermined highs and lows 104–9
shooting star candlesticks 100–2
timescales 103–4, 185–97
useful predetermined pivot lines 99–100
uses 99–102, 115–17, 150–1, 180–97
weekly charts 102–4, 182–97
polarity concepts 2–3, 75, 88–90, 113–24
  see also support and resistance levels
practical applications 3, 179–97
predetermined pivot highs and lows 104–9
professional investors
  recommendations 195–6
  trending environment 136–7, 195–6
projection levels, Fibonacci levels 111–19

rabbits, ducks 195–6
recommendations, critique 195–6
resistance levels
  see also support. . .
  concepts 2–3, 7, 8–11, 14, 16–18, 28, 30, 38, 47–8, 50–2, 63, 85–124, 127–30, 155–9, 165–77, 179–97
  definition 89
  support becomes resistance 88–90
retracement levels, Fibonacci levels 111–19, 138–9, 176–7, 180–97
return moves 63
reversal patterns 2, 28, 32, 53–4, 66, 67–84, 86–124, 138–9, 155–9, 168–77
  see also individual patterns; patterns
  concepts 66, 67–84, 138–9, 155–9, 168–77
  critique 83–4
risk/reward ratios 192–3, 196
Roman architecture, Fibonacci ratios 110–11
RSI oscillator
  see also momentum. . .
  concepts 125, 140–3, 147–8, 154–9, 180–97
  definition 140–1
  stochastic contrasts 142–3
  uses 140–1, 180–97

selling 2–3, 7, 8–9, 16–20, 52, 85–124, 140–59, 161–77, 179–97
    see also exit. . .; shadows
shadows 4–7, 8–52, 54, 100–24
    see also buying. . .; selling. . .
shooting star candlesticks
    concepts 13, 14, 20–2, 47–8, 100–2
    definition 14, 20
    pivot lines 100–2
short legs, foreign exchange swaps 199
short-term charts
    concepts 3, 10–14, 28, 50–2, 88–90, 96–100, 107–10, 129–30, 135–6, 144–5, 161–2, 167–8, 172–7, 184–97
    entry/exit issues 161–2, 167–8, 172–7, 184–97
    Japanese candlesticks 172–7, 184–97
    patterns 174–7, 184–97
short-term time horizons, trend lines 90, 96–100, 172–7, 184–97
signals
    see also Japanese candlesticks
    concepts 1–52, 85–6, 162–77, 179–97
    double signals 32–52
    MACD-Histogram 146–59, 173–5
    single signals 7–32
simple moving averages (SMAs)
    see also moving averages
    calculations 127–9, 170–7
    channels 132–9, 158–9, 188–97
    concepts 125–39, 147–8, 158–9, 173–7, 180–97
    definition 125–6
    timescales 127–8, 173–7
    uses 125–33, 158–9, 180–97
single signals, Japanese candlesticks 7–32
slippage problems 177
SMAs *see* simple moving averages
software downloads, practice 197
spike patterns *see* 'V' reversal patterns
spinning top candlesticks
    concepts 13, 14, 24–5, 49–52, 120–4, 153–4
    definitions 14, 24
spot gold markets 60, 113–14
spot transactions, definition 200

standard day candlesticks
    concepts 13, 14, 24, 26, 155–9
    definition 14, 24
standard line candlesticks
    concepts 13, 14, 24, 26, 155–9
    definition 14, 24
stochastic oscillator 5–7, 125, 141–6, 152–9, 180–97
    see also momentum. . .
    concepts 141–6, 152–9, 180–97
    definition 141–2
    parameters 142–3
    RSI contrasts 142–3
stop-loss orders 7, 77, 86, 93–4, 108–10, 166–70, 173–5, 193–7
strategies 2, 3, 83–4, 161–77, 179–97
    break outs 83–4, 167–8
    concepts 2, 3, 83–4, 167–8
    patterns 83–4, 161–77, 179–97
support and resistance levels
    see also polarity concepts
    concepts 2–3, 7, 8–9, 14, 16–18, 24, 27, 32, 34, 38, 43, 47–8, 52, 63, 66, 75, 85–124, 127–39, 150–1, 155–9, 161–77, 179–97
    critique 123–4
    definitions 88–90
    Fibonacci levels 85–6, 110–19, 124, 138–9, 176–7, 180–97
    intermediate trend lines 85–6, 95–8, 99–100, 117–19, 120–4, 135–9, 147–8, 167, 172–3, 179–97
    moving averages 127–39, 155–9, 180–97
    pivot lines 2–3, 7, 16–18, 52, 66, 75, 85–6, 96–110, 124, 137–9, 150–1, 155–9, 180–97
    support becomes resistance 88–90
    trend lines 2–3, 4–52, 53–84, 85–124, 133–9, 147–8, 167, 172–3, 179–97
swaps
    see also currency. . .; foreign exchange. . .; interest rate. . .
    concepts 199–200

technical analysis 1–52, 85–6, 124, 152–9, 179–97
    see also chart. . .

Index

final word 186–7
overview of the book 1–3, 196–7
technical plans
  see also strategies
  concepts 2, 3, 179–97
  development considerations 194–7
timescales
  continuation patterns 84
  moving averages 127–31, 173–7
  pivot lines 103–4, 185–97
  trend lines 90
tops 20, 28, 38
trading plans
  see also strategies
  concepts 2, 3, 179–97
  development considerations 194–7
trend lines 2–3, 4–52, 53–84, 85–124,
  133–9, 147–8, 167, 172–3, 179–97
  see also continuation patterns
  break of trend lines 94–5
  channels 90–5
  concepts 2–3, 4–52, 84, 85–124, 179–97
  intermediate trend lines 85–6, 95–8,
    99–100, 117–19, 120–4, 135–9, 147–8,
    167, 172–3, 180–97
  internal trend lines 96, 99, 122–4
  long-term time horizons 50–2, 77, 90–1,
    93–4, 96–9, 114–15, 128–39, 167–8
  market angle gradient 94–5
  medium-term time horizons 90
  professional investors 136–7, 195–6
  short-term time horizons 90, 96–100,
    172–7, 184–97
  time horizons 90
triangles 5–7, 57, 60–3, 120–4, 166–7, 196
triple bottom reversal patterns
  concepts 69, 73, 155–9
  definition 69
triple top reversal patterns
  concepts 69, 71
  definition 69
turning points 43, 125–59
tweezer bottom candlesticks 38, 52, 56, 89,
  117–19, 120–4, 134, 136–7, 153–4,
  173, 185–90

concepts 38, 52
definition 38
variations 38
tweezer dark cloud cover candlesticks
  38, 40
tweezer engulfing candlesticks 38, 40–1,
  189–90
tweezer harami candlesticks 38, 40
tweezer top candlesticks 38, 40, 47–8,
  49–51, 52, 56, 89, 117–19, 120–4, 134,
  136–7, 153–4, 173, 185–90
  concepts 38, 40, 47–8, 49–51, 52
  definition 38
  variations 38, 40

USD/CAD 7, 19, 31, 40, 48, 80, 88, 92, 94,
  113, 164, 170, 171, 180–4
USD/CHF 17, 21, 61, 63, 175, 180–1
USD/JPY 18, 23, 41, 42, 44, 56, 65, 71, 73,
  76, 78–9, 94, 107–8, 116, 118–19,
  130–1, 133, 136–7, 149, 151, 164, 185,
  186, 191, 192, 195

'V' reversal patterns
  see also bearish. . .; bullish. . .
  concepts 72–7, 78–9, 163
  definition 72, 76
volumes
  concepts 3, 161–5, 175–7, 180–97
  entry/exit issues 161–5, 175–7,
    180–97

'W' patterns *see* triple. . .
watch lists 190–7
weekly charts 12, 17, 19, 21, 44, 45, 46, 50,
  51, 76, 79, 81, 88, 99, 102–4, 111, 117,
  126, 145, 173, 179–97
  see also individual currencies
  pivot lines 102–4, 182–97
  practical applications 179–97
  uses 50, 51, 179–97
white Japanese candlesticks, concepts
  8–52
wicks 52
Wilder, J.Wells, Jr 140

Index compiled by Terry Halliday